The FROEBEL EDUCATIONAL INSTITUTE:
the Origins and History of the College

CW00673581

PETER WESTON

University of Surrey Roehampton

Notes on Nomenclature

- The Froebel Educational Institute [FEI] was never just a college. It was planned as a Training College with an integral Demonstration School (sometimes called the Model School) and a Practising School (originally planned to be a Free School). The Principal of the College was responsible to the FEI Committee (originally called Executive Committee) and managed the Headmistresses of the Schools. Staff often taught at both College and School(s). In fact the Practising School was never integral and never free, though fees were low.

- The Schools were referred to sometimes as 'Kindergarten and School' and sometimes as 'School'. (They took children from 3 to 14.) I have used either term as appropriate to the context.

- The first location of FEI was 'Colet Gardens, Talgarth Road', and was sometimes referred to as Colet Gardens, sometimes as Talgarth Road. I have used Colet Gardens, though the part of Colet Gardens in which it was located was renamed 'Talgarth Road' when the Hammersmith Flyover was constructed. It was strictly speaking in West Kensington, though was sometimes referred to as in Hammersmith. I have used West Kensington.

- FEI was incorporated in 1900 as a 'company not for gain' under licence from the Board of Trade. It was thereafter known either as FEI or IFEI. I have normally used FEI.

- Mr Claude Goldsmid-Montefiore was generally called Mr Montefiore, even though he himself added his mother's maiden name (Goldsmid) to his surname by deed poll. He was awarded honorary doctorates in 1921 and 1927 from Manchester and Oxford, and was sometimes called Dr, but more often just Mr.

- Until the 1960s staff were generally known by surnames, and I have followed this convention after the first mention. So, normally, Mme Michaelis, rather than Emilie Michaelis, Miss Lawrence rather than Esther Lawrence, Miss Jebb rather than Eglantyne Jebb, but Molly Brearley rather than Miss Brearley.

Cover: The library at Colet Gardens
Inside cover: The FEI crest, introduced in 1931
The Author: Dr Peter Weston is Principal of Froebel College and Pro-Rector (Academic) at University of Surrey Roehampton

Designed by FACE

University of Surrey Roehampton, 2002
ISBN 1902743 45 8

CONTENTS

The Froebel Movement is a term loosely used to refer to the activities of a group of persons committed to the development and spread of that set of educational principles and values which found their first embodiment in the kindergarten. By the later nineteenth century the kindergarten had become an internationally recognised institution.

The Froebel Educational Institute, of which Froebel College is a part, grew out of that movement. It owed its foundation in 1892 and its survival to the idealism, determination and commitment of several people, of whom two in particular deserve special notice. One was the wealthy, philanthropic widow of an émigré German industrialist who had settled in Manchester, Mrs Julia Salis-Schwabe, and the other was an internationally distinguished scholar of progressive liberal views, Dr Claude Montefiore.

However, the full story leading to the foundation of the College begins some half-century earlier in Thuringia, central Germany.

ONE

Friedrich Froebel (1782-1852)

Friedrich Fröbel auf dem Wege nach Keilhau

WHEN Friedrich Froebel died, in 1852 at the age of 70, he must have thought that his whole life's work was in ruins. In 1805 he had, almost by chance, had his first experience of teaching a class of pupils in a progressive school in Frankfurt. A few weeks later he had visited the renowned educationist Pestalozzi in Yverdon in Switzerland, and on his return to Frankfurt had written to his brother that 'my life has at last discovered its native element'. By the 1830s, working in Switzerland, he had come to realise, contrary to accepted belief, that the most important period for learning was the *pre-school* period. He followed Rousseau in believing that children actually *want* to learn, and that effective learning is through activity, which is commonly called 'play' at this age. Learning through activity is a holistic process which, he argued, adults should treat with respect, because in childhood is established the foundation for all subsequent learning.

In 1837, having developed and tested a radically new educational method and philosophy based on structured, activity-based learning with sequences of toys, games, songs and dances, Froebel moved to Bad Blankenburg, near Weimar, and shortly afterwards established there his first *Play and Activity Institute,* which he renamed in 1840 *kindergarten*. This differentiated it from 'school', which had very different connotations – and very different methods of 'instruction' at that time. The name 'kindergarten' signifies both a garden *for* children, a location where they can observe and interact with nature, and also a garden *of* children, where they themselves can grow and develop in freedom from arbitrary political and social imperatives. The kindergarten 'system' was

The first kindergarten at Bad Blankenburg

The garden at Bad Blankenburg

essentially tri-partite: toys for sedentary creative play (these Froebel called 'gifts' and 'occupations'), games and dances for healthy activity, and observing and nurturing plants in a garden for stimulating awareness of the natural world. The whole system was articulated and justified by Froebel in the language of the German idealist philosophy of the early decades of the century, with a Christian inflexion. It was a search for metaphysical 'unity', in which the potential growth to 'wholeness' of the individual child within the natural world would fulfil a harmonious ideal within the mind of God. This became both a strength of the 'Froebel movement', as the language generated a sense of quasi-religious mission, but also, as time went on and more pragmatic imperatives for universal education asserted themselves, it became a weakness. Metaphysical notions became inaccessible and old-fashioned to all but a diminishing band of believers.

For the next eleven years, through his sixties, Froebel worked tirelessly in promoting the kindergarten system. He lobbied local officials and parents all over the German

states, and by 1850 sixteen had been established, together with a number of training centres for young women as 'kindergartners'. He was instinctively a supporter of the political revolution which swept Germany and much of Europe in 1848. He believed in 'republican virtues', and like many other members of the liberal middle class, saw the scores of semi-feudal German states as in desperate need of modernisation in the face of industrialisation and all its social changes. More than just that, however, Froebel's rejection of state authoritarianism in favour of play and creative imagination was a truly radical vision for humanity which would almost inevitably put his work in jeopardy.

A breakthrough for the kindergarten movement came in 1850 when the Duke of Meiningen donated one of his residences, a splendid hunting lodge at Marienthal, as a centre for the training of kindergartners. This was one of the first training institutes for women, as it was Froebel's view that women should be trained to become the 'educators of humanity'. Almost immediately, however, there followed a fatal blow to the movement. On 7

Marienthal Hunting Lodge, where Froebel set up his training college for kindergartners, and where he died two years later, in 1852

who were committed to Froebel's ideals moved abroad – to England, Ireland, and many other countries of Europe, as well as the USA. The kindergarten itself had become an icon of liberal progressive values. Baroness Bertha von Marenholtz-Bülow, who had met Froebel first in 1849, when she was 33, and thereafter became his most ardent propagandist until her death in 1893, had known or trained many of the 'disciples' who established kindergartens and training courses abroad.

August 1851 the Prussian government passed a repressive decree (the *Kindergartenverbot*) requiring the closure of all kindergartens, fearing that their liberal education system, based on encouraging the free development of children's faculties, was a contributory factor to the radicalism which had supposedly led to revolution and threatened to topple the government. Bavaria followed suit in November and other German

states and Swiss cantons followed thereafter. Froebel died less than a year later, in June 1852, severely dejected, but still convinced of the rightness of his cause and of its ultimate triumph.

Repressive and totalitarian measures, however, often have unexpected results. Many German kindergartners

Baroness Bertha von Marenholtz-Bülow

TWO

The Froebel Movement in England

THE first significant kindergarten in England was established in 1851 by a young woman in her twenties, Mme Bertha Ronge (née Meyer). The Meyers were a prominent Hamburg family, and Bertha and her younger sister Margarethe had met Froebel in Hamburg in 1849 and been trained by him in kindergarten principles. Their kindergarten was well established in Tavistock Place, central London, by 1854. (Margarethe, with her husband Carl Schurz, then moved on to Watertown, Wisconsin, where they established the first kindergarten in the USA in 1856.) In 1857 one of Bertha Ronge's former trainees opened a kindergarten in Manchester, and in 1873 a group of émigré Froebelians founded the Manchester Kindergarten Association, the first in England. Others soon followed. Manchester became a strong centre of kindergarten activity, supported by the presence of a large number of German and (often) Jewish industrial entrepreneurs who lived in the city. Two notable figures in the Manchester Kindergarten Association were Miss Eleonore Heerwart and Mme Adele de Portugall.

Miss Heerwart had worked at Keilhau in Froebel's first school, and had in the early 1850s established a kindergarten in Dublin. She arrived in Manchester in 1861 to lecture on kindergarten theory and practice. In 1874 she became Principal of Stockwell Training College in London (founded by the British & Foreign School Society).

Mme de Portugall was the widow of an East Prussian nobleman, who put all her energies into the Froebelian movement. She had worked with Baroness von Bülow in Germany, and ran a kindergarten in Manchester from

1861-63. She then moved to Switzerland, eventually moving to Geneva, where the canton became the first state in the world formally to adopt and to implement Froebel's principles as the basis of the education system. Finally, in 1884, she moved to Naples, where she was appointed by her old friend from Manchester, Mme Salis-Schwabe, to run the Naples kindergartens which she had originally established.

From the point of view of the establishment of FEI, the most important name from Manchester is Mme Julia Salis-Schwabe. (Her mother's name was Salis and her father's Schwabe.) She was not a kindergarten teacher

Portrait of Julia Salis-Schwabe, painted by Ari Scheffer in 1850, when she was 31

or educational theorist. Originally from Bremen, she had married her cousin in 1837 at the age of 18 (he was 36). Both were part of a large German-Jewish population in Manchester in the first half of the nineteenth century, many of whom, including the Schwabes, took up British citizenship.

The Schwabe household was Unitarian, and became a centre of enlightened Liberalism. Unitarians believed that social evils were the result of human action, not of original sin, and therefore that they could be remedied by human effort. They were advocates of democracy, or at least of encouraging working men, by hard work, thrift and education, to achieve the franchise. Congregations grew in large industrial centres such as Manchester, where the relatively small membership included prominent names in industry, such as the Wedgwoods, Courtaulds, and Tates. Friends and visitors at the Schwabe house included not only Richard Cobden and John Bright, the radicals, but also the renowned singer Jenny Lind and Frederic Chopin. The latter, visiting in 1848, found Herr Schwabe's playing on the piano 'distinguished for great delicacy and sentiment', and thought his wife to be 'particularly kind'. Herr Schwabe's factories near Manchester were renowned as models of progressive social action, providing schools for employees' children, as well as other social benefits. He gave £25,000 to build a mental home in Manchester in order to stop the chaining and beating which was then common in lunatic asylums. Julia Salis-Schwabe enjoyed a well-connected, wealthy, philanthropic and cultured background.

Mme Salis-Schwabe was widowed in 1853, aged 34, and was left with seven children – and a large fortune. The

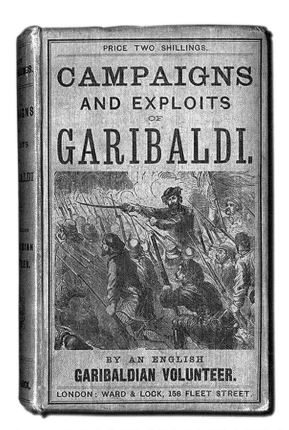

One of many accounts of Garibaldi published in England in the 1860s, by W.B. Brooke (1861)

close friendship with the Cobdens had led Julia Salis-Schwabe to share a dream of international understanding and peace. She had discovered the Froebelian system during her travels in the German states with her husband and Cobden, and she came to see Froebel's philosophy, with its practical system for developing the physical, mental and moral powers in children as the key to social progress. This would, she believed, be the foundation of international understanding. She devoted her considerable energies, influence and wealth to its promotion, until her death in May 1896.

At this time, in mid-Victorian England, Garibaldi was idealised as a heroic, romantic patriot-leader, particularly after his capture of Naples and the proclamation of the Kingdom of Italy in 1860-61. Julia Salis-Schwabe organised supplies for Garibaldi's 'Thousand Redshirts', and, moved by the desperate plight of slum children in Naples, collected appeal funds and established a school there in 1861. She saw education, rather than mere charity, as the answer to the problem of poverty, breaking the cycle of destitution. She returned eight years later, purchased a disused medical college in the city and established there in 1873 a free kindergarten, elementary school and orphanage, despite continued opposition from the Roman Catholic priesthood. The Queen of Italy became its patron. A fee-paying school for children of the middle classes and a training college were added later. By 1890 over 10,000 pupils had passed through the doors of the establishment. (It was said by the then Italian Minister of Education, Professor Pasquale Villari, that 'she travelled second-class in Italy and third-class in England for economy's sake and for the benefit of the Poor School in Naples'.) The once-derided utopian scheme had become self-supporting, as a result of the income from a large endowment from Julia Salis-Schwabe, together with fee income and an annual grant from the Italian Government, and became named by Royal Decree *Istituto Froebeliano Internazionale Vittorio Emmanuele II.*

Julia Salis-Schwabe later expounded her philosophy in an address to the International Educational Congress in Brussels in 1880, in which she said

The only true liberty is to be free of human passions and worldly prejudices, and to respect the opinions of others as we wish ours to be respected…The troubles of the present day are but the natural consequence of imperfect and, in many cases, depraved commercial, political and social morality, and this arises, in a great degree, from the want of education in first principles…There is as much mischief done and misery caused by sheer ignorance and want of reasoning powers as by malice.

With its Victorian resonance, this could stand as a rationale for the Froebel movement at the time.

During the 1860s, following the revocation of the ban on kindergartens by the Prussian government, many of the leading proponents of kindergartens began to return to Germany. The Froebel movement in England was in danger of stalling: its image was foreign, its leaders were leaving the country, and recruits for training were hard to find. Two developments saved the situation.

The first was the passing of the Elementary Education Act in 1870 (the 'Forster' Act), which gave some impetus to the shrinking Froebel movement. The Act introduced universal elementary education, thus establishing the first national system of education in England and Wales. It required the establishment of elected School Boards, which had the authority to build and maintain 'Board Schools' at the expense of the ratepayers. Attendance by children between the ages of 5 and 10 was made compulsory in 1880, and payment of any fees was abolished in 1891. The London School Board soon started introducing educational innovations, such as separate classrooms for each age-group, a central hall for whole-school activities and specialist rooms for practical

Maria Grey (1815-1906)

purpose for which they were designed, nevertheless here was an opportunity for a different attitude to children's learning to establish itself universally in the public sector. It would take many years.

The second was the establishment in 1872 by prominent figures in the women's movement, including the sisters Maria Grey and Emily Shirreff, of the Girls' Public Day School Company (now the Girls' Day School Trust). Their aim was 'to promote the establishment of good and cheap day-schools, for all classes above those attending the public elementary schools' (*Prospectus*, 1871). Within six years seventeen schools had been established, many with a kindergarten. (Today there are 25 GDST schools, with 19,500 pupils.) Until the 1870s few daughters of the professional and business classes had trained as teachers, as their parents were unwilling to send them to the largely working class environment of the church training colleges and elementary schools. Now these parents had a further choice for their daughters, in addition to the roles of governess or nurse-maid. As they reached school-leaving age, many helped out in the kindergartens of their schools, and thus a supply of training recruits was produced. The kindergarten became anglicised and eminently respectable. (The kindergarten training colleges of the British & Foreign Schools Society, at Stockwell and Saffron Walden, by contrast, targeted students from the respectable working-class.)

In April 1874, Mme Emilie Michaelis came to England, having worked in kindergartens in Switzerland and Italy. She was forty years old, the daughter of the court physician in Gotha, Thuringia. She had known Baroness

activities. In this context there was a chance for the Froebel movement to influence the whole national education system. Even though pictures survive of serried ranks of children each copying the teacher in manipulating gifts 2-4 (the blocks – see p.53), which was quite in ignorance of the freely creative child-centred

von Bülow since 1863, when she had attended some of her lectures in Berlin, and she also knew Julia Salis-Schwabe through the same connection. Later to become the first Principal of Froebel College, she came first to set up a kindergarten in Notting Hill High School (a GPDSCo school), and was then invited to lecture to Croydon School Board teachers about kindergarten methods. By January 1875 she had jointly founded the renowned Croydon Kindergarten, which in 1880 became the Croydon Kindergarten Company, Ltd., with herself as its Headmistress. In 1889 she was back in Notting Hill, as Principal of 'The Frœbel Training School of Primary Instruction' in Norland Place. (This Training School had been set up by Mrs Walter Ward, who in 1892 also founded the Norland Institute, which went on to train the uniformed 'Norland Nannies' thereafter – a quite separate form of training for working with young children.) Within four years the Froebel Training School was to move to West Kensington to form the nucleus of Froebel College, with Emilie Michaelis as its first Principal, on the invitation of Julia Salis-Schwabe.

Mme Emilie Michaelis in 1870

opposite: Prospectus of the Frœbel Training School, Norland Place

THE FRŒBEL TRAINING SCHOOL

OF PRIMARY INSTRUCTION.

Principal = = MADAME MICHAELIS.

11, Norland Place, Holland Park Gardens, Uxbridge Road, W.

THE FRŒBEL TRAINING SCHOOL provides Instruction for those who wish to become educators of children.

The various subjects included under the head of Primary Instruction will be taught by means of Lectures and Model Lessons; in addition to this a full Kindergarten Training will be given.

The Training School is intended for two classes of Students:

(*a*) Girls above the age of 16, who have already obtained some qualifying English certificate, and who are wishing to pass the Elementary or lower examination of the Joint Board of the Frœbel Society.

(*b*) Girls above the age of 17, who are desirous of passing the higher examination of the Joint Board, and who have already passed the Elementary Examination or who possess the necessary English certificate.

N.B.—Students who have not passed an English examination may be prepared at the College for the Lower Preliminary Certificate of the Joint Board. Fees £5 5s. for One Term.

THREE

The Froebel Society

BY 1874, several figures who were to become notable in the English Froebel movement had arrived in or remained in England and established kindergartens, but there was as yet, outside Manchester, no coordinating organisation through which experiences could be shared and practice enhanced. There was no national organisation. Miss Doreck, later to become the first President of the Froebel Society, had come to England in 1857 and by 1870 was running a very successful kindergarten in Kensington. One November evening in 1874, she invited a group of a dozen young women who were practising kindergarten teachers to her house at 63 Kensington Gardens Square, to consider the establishment of a formal association, which it was agreed would be called 'Fröbel Society for the Promotion of the Kindergarten System'. Those present included Miss Heerwart, from Stockwell Training College, two sisters, Maria Grey (after whom a London Training College was named, which survived independently until 1976), her sister Emily Shirreff (who wrote on Froebel and edited his letters), Mme Michaelis, and Emily Lord (later known as Mrs Walter Ward), a young teacher at Notting Hill High School when Emilie

Michaelis was appointed. The Society was established, with Miss Doreck as its first President, and invitations were sent out inviting applications for membership. Miss Doreck died within a few months, in June 1875, and Emily Shirreff was elected President, and her sister, Maria Grey, Vice-President.

The Society spent much of its first two years in clarifying its own philosophy through lectures and discussions of Froebel's educational principles, but then

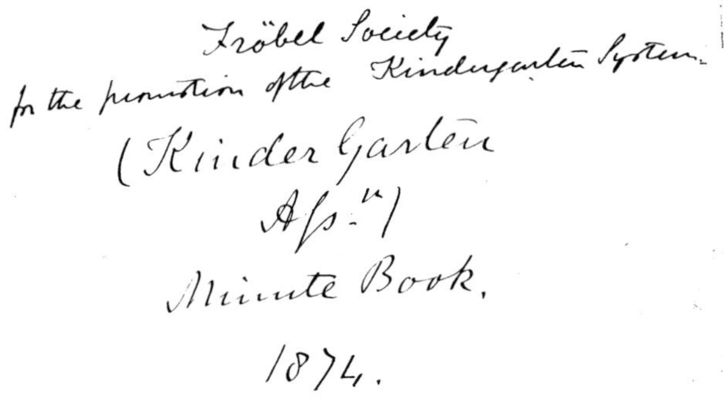

Caption text from handwritten document:

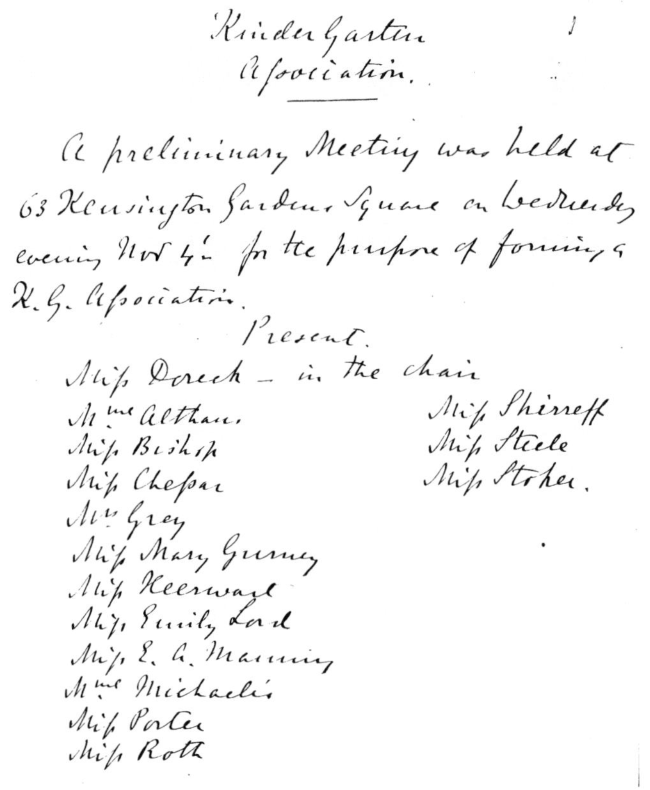

Kinder Garten Association.

A preliminary Meeting was held at 63 Kensington Gardens Square on Wednesday evening Nov 4th for the purpose of forming a K.G. Association.

Present.

Miss Doreck — in the chair
Mme Althaus, Miss Bishop, Miss Chepae, Mr Grey, Miss Mary Gurney, Miss Heerwart, Miss Emily Lord, Miss E. A. Manning, Mme Michaelis, Miss Porter, Miss Roth
Miss Shirreff, Miss Steele, Miss Stoher

Fröbel Society for the promotion of the Kindergarten System. (Kinder Garten Ass.") Minute Book. 1874.

From the Minutes of the first meeting of the Froebel Society by 1877 moved on to raising funds for the establishment of a central Kindergarten Training College in London, as general understanding of Froebelian principles and practice was very poor, even in training colleges. Eventually after intensive fund-raising efforts, mainly through drawing-room meetings, on 3 May 1879 the 'Kindergarten Training College' was opened at 31 Tavistock Place with ten students, under the principalship of Miss Caroline Bishop, who had been the first lecturer on Kindergarten methods appointed to the London School Board. This could be regarded as the first 'Froebel College' in England.

However, the finances were not sound, and it did not last. Membership of the Froebel Society was dwindling, mainly because it still worked almost entirely in the private and charitable sectors and depended almost entirely on membership fees for survival. The Manchester Kindergarten Association was still not affiliated. When a resolution at the monthly meeting of the Froebel Society was carried to celebrate the centenary of the birth of Froebel in 1882 by establishing a free Kindergarten for poor children in London, it was shelved because of lack of funds. Likewise, the following year, when the Training College asked the Society for financial support, it was not forthcoming. The College was obliged to close. Within a few months the very existence of the Froebel Society was under threat, when the Secretary resigned, in early 1884.

The Society resolved itself into a Council in 1884, to which, following an introduction by Julia Salis-Schwabe who was a friend of his mother, a young man of 26 was elected. His name was Claude Goldsmid Montefiore,

and he had only three years before come down from Balliol College, Oxford, where he had taken first class honours in Classics. His maternal grandfather, Sir Isaac Goldsmid, had been the first Jewish Lord Mayor of London and one of the founders of University College London, and of the West London (Reform) Synagogue, and his father was the nephew of Sir Moses Montefiore, the great philanthropist and advocate of Jewish rights. (It was only twenty-six years earlier, in 1858, the year of Claude Montefiore's birth, that an Act of Parliament had been passed to allow Jews to stand as MPs, and it was still unusual for them to attend the ancient universities, even after the Universities Tests Act of 1871, which removed the legal barriers.) Claude Montefiore had been in Berlin following his graduation, and it was there that he had encountered the Froebel movement for the first time. He was now to become continuously and actively associated with the Froebel movement, and Froebel College in particular, until his death fifty-four years later, in 1938.

Though inclined towards the life of a scholar, he believed that he should not stay aloof from the real struggles against the social evils of his time, and he devoted his considerable wealth (inherited following the deaths of his uncle, brother and father between 1878 and 1883) and his time and energy to the support of FEI, while maintaining a very distinguished scholarly output of lectures, articles and books. These included most notably his unique and controversial two-volume commentary on the synoptic Gospels from the perspective of Judaism, first published in 1909. During that same time also he was to become effectively the founder of the Liberal Jewish movement in England, an internationally distinguished scholar in the field of liberal theology and Biblical criticism, and President of University College Southampton (later to become the University of Southampton) from 1915 to 1934. He was a fervent anti-Zionist, while calling himself 'a die-hard Jew'. His values were, like those of the Unitarians, entirely universalist, and he was co-founder with the Roman Catholic scholar, Baron von Hügel, of the ecumenical London Society for the Study of Religion, which was established to promote understanding and rapprochement between different faiths.

Almost immediately Claude Montefiore became Secretary to the Society. Intensive publicity and fund-raising efforts were started. Discussions were opened with the Manchester Kindergarten Association and the Bedford Kindergarten Association about joint recognition and approval of kindergartens and about possible amalgamation. Anxiety about the dangers to the movement from imperfectly trained teachers led to the formation of the National Froebel Union in 1887, which became the body responsible for approving syllabi, setting examinations, and issuing Teacher's Certificates to trainees. The centralised control of the authorised Froebel's Teacher's Certificate was jealously guarded, in order to discredit the pseudo-qualifications being issued by teachers who had no sound knowledge of Froebelian philosophy or methods.

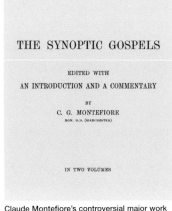

THE SYNOPTIC GOSPELS

EDITED WITH
AN INTRODUCTION AND A COMMENTARY
BY
C. G. MONTEFIORE
HON. D.D. (MANCHESTER)

IN TWO VOLUMES

Claude Montefiore's controversial major work

Claude Montefiore

Claude Montefiore had married Therese Schorstein, granddaughter of a Polish rabbi, in 1886, by whom he had a son, Leonard, who was to succeed him in his commitment to FEI many years later. Sadly Therese died in childbirth in 1889. There was to be a second marriage without issue some years later, to a Jewish convert, Florence Ward, who was Vice-Mistress of Girton College, Cambridge.

1892: The Proposal and Constitution for a Froebel Educational Institute

Julia Salis-Schwabe

vision for England. Now 71 years old and having returned from her successful enterprise in Naples, she declares three aims in the first Prospectus for a 'Froebel Educational Institute':

1. To prove to the British Public...that the principles laid down by Froebel, the distinguished founder of the Kindergarten system, are capable of further adoption and extension to the higher stages of education beyond the Infant School...;
2. to show that Froebel's principles and methods...are especially adapted to meet the admitted necessities of the educational system of an industrial people such as that of Great Britain;
3. to increase the provision of the necessary teachers.

An anonymous article in the Queen of 23 April 1892 noted:

Mrs Salis Schwabe's aim is not merely to supply London with a free Kindergarten. A single free Kindergarten would go a very little way among the children of London. Mrs Schwabe's aim is rather to establish an institution which will make its mark upon elementary education as a whole, and lead to the general adoption of better principles in elementary schools. In this country the only means of making a reform "actual" is to show it at work.

The article refers to the 'specially British delusion' that the 'three r's' were an adequate education for the young', and continues:

If the finished product of the board school uses one of the three r's for the perusal of sporting tips and penny

BY 1890, the Froebel movement in England was increasingly vigorous. There were the now well-established Froebel Society, which promoted Froebelian philosophy and methods, the National Froebel Union, which set standards and issued teacher's certificates, and substantial training centres (including Maria Grey College, Bedford Training College, and Stockwell College). Mrs Julia Salis Schwabe had a larger

dreadfuls, if he uses the second to write up his betting book, and the third to cast up the odds, can any reasonable person say that he is better off with his new accomplishments than he was without them?

What the Froebel system produced, by contrast, the article continued, was 'the development of intelligence, the training simultaneously of hand, eye and brain, the encouragement of good taste and right feeling – all this and more'.

THE

FROEBEL EDUCATIONAL INSTITUTE.

Colêt Gardens, West Kensington, London, W.

President - - - -	MRS. SALIS SCHWABE.
Chairman of Committee -	MR. W. MATHER, M.P.
Treasurer - - - -	MR. C. G. MONTEFIORE.
Secretary - - - -	MR. ARTHUR G. SYMONDS, M.A.

THE TRAINING COLLEGE FOR TEACHERS.

Principal = = MADAME MICHAELIS,

WHO IS ASSISTED BY A STAFF OF COMPETENT TRAINERS AND TEACHERS.

THE COLLEGE provides Training for those who wish to become educators of children in Kindergartens, Schools, and Private Families.

The Training will be given by means of Lectures and Model Lessons, and will also include a course of Practice under Supervision.

The new Institute

14

It was from this crucible of late Victorian benevolence – a synergy between liberal thought and private wealth – that FEI was to emerge. The somewhat patronising rhetoric revealed a fear of the increasingly numerous and politically active urban proletariat, with their betting and penny dreadfuls, but it was hoped, in accordance with positive Liberal principles, that in an 'industrial nation' with 'good taste and right feeling' everything would be all right.

It should be remembered that life for working-class children was still extremely grim in the 1890s. Mayhew in the 1860s had deplored 'the precocity of the youth of both sexes in London', whose 'drinking, smoking, blasphemy, indecency and immorality…does not even call up a blush', and had commented that the 'charity schools and the spread of education do not seem to have done much to abate this scourge'. The 'progressive' Factory Act of 1891 had raised the minimum age at which a child could be set to work from ten to eleven, but this could be for ten working hours a day. Margaret McMillan, a lifelong campaigner for improvement in the conditions of children together with her sister Rachel, visited Bradford for the first time in 1892, and commented later (in 1927):

The condition of the poorer children was worse than anything that was described or painted…The neglect of infants, the utter neglect almost of toddlers and older children, the blight of early labour, all combined to make of a once vigorous people a race of undergrown and spoiled adolescents…just as people looked on at the torture two hundred years ago and less, without any great indignation, so in the 1890s people saw the misery of poor children without any great perturbation.

In this context Julia Salis-Schwabe's energy, courage and determination were extraordinary and inspiring. In unambiguous language she declares:

We intend, therefore, in this Institute to give a practical living exposition of the value of Froebel's principles in every stage of education; and we do this in the firm conviction that the matter is of the greatest national importance; for on the right training of the young depends the continuous progress of our country. We propose to erect two Model Kindergartens and Schools, one paying and the other free, on either side of the College, as is shown in the illustration. [see p.20]

She called a meeting on 22 October 1892 in the Westminster Palace Hotel, at which the Froebel Educational Institute was constituted, and a Council and Executive Committee appointed to raise funds, secure premises, set up a Training College and Model Kindergarten, and appoint a Principal. Julia Salis-Schwabe herself became President of the FEI, Claude Montefiore became Treasurer, and William Mather became Chairman.

William Mather (later, in 1902, Sir William) was an old friend of the Schwabes, like them a Liberal in politics and benevolent employer, owner of a large engineering works in Manchester. Born in 1838, he was twenty years older than Claude Montefiore. He had become an apprentice in his father's factory at the age of 12, at the age of 30 had taken control of the firm, Mather & Platt. He first entered parliament in 1885. He travelled the world in developing his business, and was notable for installing the first electric traction on a railway in England – the City and South London underground line,

education was the key to freedom, democracy and national progress. He was to found the Mather Training College in Manchester, but never lost interest in FEI. He was awarded three honorary doctorates, from Bristol, Manchester, and Princeton universities, during his life. He was a kind, generous and genial man, and from its inception maintained a close interest in FEI, at one time in 1910 hiring charabancs to bring the whole college down for a day's outing to his home, Bramshaw, in the New Forest. He remained Chairman until 1917, when he withdrew as a result of ill-health and Claude Montefiore was appointed to replace him. He then accepted the title of President, which he held for three years until his death in 1920.

Julia Salis-Schwabe also managed to secure as Patroness of the emergent FEI the services of Her Imperial Majesty the Dowager Empress Frederick (1840-1901), the first child of Queen Victoria, who had married the Crown Prince of Prussia, was widowed in 1888, and was the mother of Kaiser Wilhelm II (who led Germany into World War One). (For her schools in Naples, we remember, Julia Salis-Schwabe had secured the patronage of the Queen of Italy: she was socially very well-connected.)

As Principal designate, she proposed Emilie Michaelis, whose 'Frœbel Training School of Primary Instruction' in Notting Hill by 1894 had thirty students and a handful of pupils. It was agreed with Mme Michaelis that she would bring her students and pupils to form the nucleus of the new Froebel Educational Institute. Emilie Michaelis was now fifty years old, a founder-member of the Froebel Society, and a charismatic and experienced teacher.

Sir William Mather (1838-1920)

which was opened in 1890 by the Prince of Wales (later King Edward VII). He had founded and equipped the first Free Kindergarten in Britain at Salford in 1873, which became very widely known for taking in children from the poorest homes and giving them meals and baths. He also did a great deal to promote technical education, believing, like all enlightened Liberals, that

Mme Michaelis on a picnic at Cobham in the 1890s

The next two years were very busy. One of many fund-raining 'At-homes' was held on 29 June, 1894, a very hot afternoon, at the home of Mrs Leopold de Rothschild, wife of a scion of the banking family, in Piccadilly. Claude Montefiore took the chair, in William Mather's absence, and present were Julia Salis-Schwabe, Dr Percival (Head Master of Rugby School), Dr Adler (Chief Rabbi), Mr Kekewich (Secretary of the Education Department), and many other notables of the day. Resolutions were passed, cheques were written, and letters of apology were read. One of these was from the philosopher and pre-eminent Unitarian, James Martineau (1805-1900), brother of the theist feminist writer, Harriet. Writing aged 89, his words eloquently distil the essence of what the Froebel movement meant for British education. Although tinged with a certain Victorian moralism, the words are surprisingly fresh. While arguing that it is not Froebelian 'animating principles' (play) that make 'lazy' children, but rather the dead load of memorising, drill and 'task-work', the letter acknowledges that true learning requires some toil:

June 25th, 1894

Dear Mr Montefiore: I much regret my inability to avail myself of Mrs Leopold de Rothschild's invitation to meet the President and Committee of the Froebel Educational Institute, having a strong conviction that our English process of elementary teaching impairs its characteristic excellences for want of certain controlling and animating principles which Froebel has rescued from neglect. We need to go back to the Socratic idea, that education is rather the development of given faculty than the imparting of absent knowledge; and is but a sleepy affair unless it proceeds by stirring the mind as well as by depositing information. Its gains are made, not by adding to the dead load upon the memory, but by fresh acts of living intelligence, every one of which quickens the growth of mental alertness. The weight of weariness, through which mere task-work makes lazy children, is lifted off by a teacher who thus keeps their thought awake. Yet his art is not the cheap device of bribing the learner by teaching him only what is entertaining and sparing him all that is

James Martineau (1805-1900) in 1887

dry and difficult. The scholar whose industry needs the bait of pleasant and tasty knowledge is foredoomed to intellectual and moral weakness. It is not the amusement received from what we learn, but the energy exercised in learning, that creates faculty to achieve and patience to endure. Without toil and drudgery the work of neither thought nor conscience can be effectually done; for training a generation that will manfully face these we must rely, not on any drill of routine, but on the constant appeal to the observing perception, the reflective intelligence, and the moral intuitions of the children whom we have to educate. ... I am, dear Sir, Very sincerely yours, James Martineau.

The Froebel Educational Institute.

THE most distinctive feature of the system of education which we employ in our Kindergarten and School is that it aims, especially during the earliest stages, rather at developing power and skill than at imparting information; though, of course, the children are enabled to acquire information as soon as ever they are ready for it. The first step is to prepare them for gaining it rightly. The system might be briefly described as the application of the laws of evolution to education, or the development of children physically, intellectually, and morally. Development, it must be borne in mind, is not so much increase of bulk or quantity as increase in complexity of structure and an improvement in power, skill, and variety in the performance of natural functions. It is produced by the proper exercise of these functions; that is, by exercises which are always rightly timed (given when needed), always in harmony with the nature of what is exercised, and continuously in proportion to its strength. In the case of children such exercises will naturally be pleasurable, and a pleasurable condition is of the greatest importance for healthy growth of all kinds. Yet it is not the pleasure or amusement derived from what we learn, but the energy exercised in learning, that creates power to achieve and patience to endure. There is, however, another point to note with regard to these exercises: they must call into activity the thing's—in our case, the child's—own natural powers; and the activity must be, as far as possible, self-produced, self-maintained, and self-directed, or, to use the ordinary term, it must be self-activity. This self-activity may be either receptive—having to do with taking in and assimilating; or creative—having to do with giving out or expressing. We lay great stress on the latter, because we hold it to be the greatest motive force in producing mental development and in effecting assimilation—the endeavour to express bringing out more distinctly the true inter-relations of what we have learnt or are learning, and impressing these on the memory. This doctrine of creativeness or expressive self-activity—including as it does all kinds of expression (movement, gesture, dramatic action, song, modelling, drawing, speech, &c.)—is one of the most valuable and interesting of all the principles which we have adopted and employ; and it has produced, and is producing, a very marked effect on contemporary education, especially in England and the United States, and in Hungary, Scandinavia and Switzerland.

Our fundamental idea is that the great aim of education should be to build up character—to produce a healthy human individuality, intelligent, possessing knowledge and able to use it, strong in purpose, reverent. To effect this we must see that the best means are supplied; we must help the young to acquire knowledge, power, and skill in the use of knowledge, and also to develop a capacity for feeling—and hereafter appreciating—all that is good and true and beautiful in life.

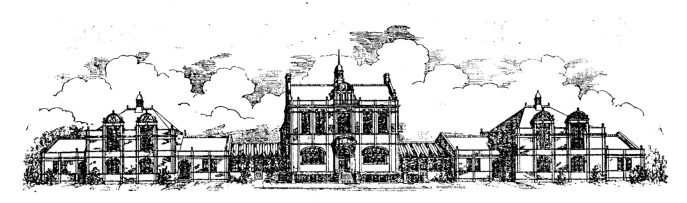

THE FROEBEL EDUCATIONAL INSTITUTE.

TALGARTH ROAD, WEST KENSINGTON.

The FEI dream – a college with a demonstration school on one side (achieved) and a free school on the other (not achieved)

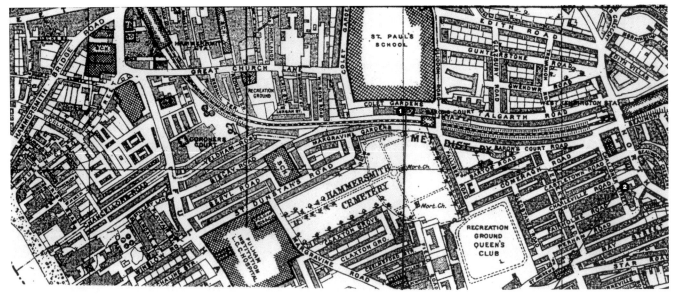

Period map showing FEI college and school (**1**.Colet Gardens/Talgarth Road) and 'low fee'd' practising school (**2**. Challoner Street)

1894: The Froebel Educational Institute becomes established

The original college building today

Miss Lawrence with a Demonstration School class at Colet Gardens

AT the end of the meeting Mr Montefiore announced that the grand total so far collected for the establishment of FEI was £6,600 (about one-seventieth of today's equivalent value). This had been enough to start on the project, but not enough to complete it. Commitment had overcome caution. A site had been found in Colet Gardens/Talgarth Road, West Kensington (now the road into which the Hammersmith Flyover spills its endless traffic, but in the 1890s a pleasant and relatively safe road). A Grand Ceremony of laying the Foundation Stone by the Dowager Empress Frederick was planned for 24 March 1894. However, an 'unexpected difficulty' had been found with taking possession of the land, and as a consequence the ceremony was postponed for a year. It was with some relief that Mr Mather sent a telegram to Julia Salis-Schwabe in Naples in January 1894, which read: 'Have signed contract today; plans and estimates preparing; building shall begin earliest moment. Nil desperandum, always follow a lady leader is the moral of our struggles, – Mather.'

The delay meant that Madame Michaelis with her (now) 66 students and 8 pupils had to move into temporary rented accommodation near to the main site. January 1895, however, saw the triumphant opening of the new College building – the central part of the planned 'Educational Institute'. The Model Kindergarten and School which were to have comprised one wing moved temporarily into two rooms of the College, under the principalship of a non-German, American-born Froebelian, Miss Esther Lawrence (who had been head of the Preparatory Department of the Chiswick High School, and was in due course to succeed Mme Michaelis as Principal of FEI). The Free Kindergarten, which was to have comprised the other wing, was still an aspiration, to which the Executive Committee attached great importance. The cost so far had been well over £7,000, and an appeal was launched for a further £10,000 so that the deficit could be filled and the two further wings built. The Executive Committee asked that original donors might consider 'a further gift of half their first donations'!

A grand celebration took place in the new College on Tuesday 5 March 1895, with the visit of the Patroness, H.I.M. The Empress Frederick, with Countess Perponcher, her Lady-in-Waiting, and Lord Hawkesbury, Lord-in-Waiting to the Queen. The Empress Frederick was introduced to the Executive Committee, the Principal, Mr Quilter the architect, and to a number of other dignitaries. Julia Salis-Schwabe was represented by her son, Colonel Schwabe, and she sent a telegram of thanks from Naples for the Empress' visit. After a conducted tour by Mr Mather, during which she observed training and kindergarten classes in progress, the Empress was escorted upstairs to hear addresses by Mr Mather MP and the Rt. Hon. A.D. Acland MP (later Sir Arthur), who was Vice-President of the Committee of Council on Education (i.e. the government's person in charge of Education). He was also a member of the FEI Governing Body.

After mentioning the need for a further £10,000 to 'build the two wings – and without those wings we cannot soar to the height of our expectations (laughter and applause)', Mr Mather said, perhaps with one eye on Mr Acland, and perhaps with the Italian Government's support of the Naples School, Kindergarten and Training College in

Demonstration School wing at Colet Gardens (damaged during WW2 and subsequently demolished)

mind, 'We cannot, perhaps, expect at once aid from Parliament for an experiment into hitherto untried channels of education. Nevertheless, the Education Department has looked upon our experiment with favour and interest…'. To which Mr Acland replied, 'We look on this effort of the Froebel Educational Institute as a most important step in advance – one of those steps which private enterprise alone can initiate, but which we shall find of great advantage in the future to the country as a whole (hear, hear, and applause).' No luck there then.

Mr Acland went on to observe that the founding of the first kindergarten by Froebel had coincided with the start of Victoria's reign, and to hope that the FEI would be fully developed and completed before the end of her reign. He expressed his further hope that 'the application of Froebel's principles would not stop when children are five or six years of age, but shall go forward until they are fifteen or sixteen', and went on to speak of the need for trained teachers 'in every rank and class of life'. He raised a laugh by referring to 'that single dread day in the year, the day of judgment, when the Inspector came' to the Board Schools, and he revealed that the Department was considering 'two or three visits…when the Inspector shall come rather as a friend' (thus reminding us that the 'payment by results' system – in force from 1862 until its abolition in 1897 – led to many teachers in many schools spending their whole time drilling their pupils in the three r's in preparation for the tests which it was the Inspector's job to administer once a year). Mr Acland concluded his address by sincerely hoping that generous contributors would be found to help the Committee to complete the two wings as speedily as possible. However, it was not to happen.

In 1896, Claude Montefiore made a personal donation of £1,000 towards the Demonstration School wing (total cost £3,700). It was opened in July 1896 by Her Royal Highness Princess Christian of Schleswig-Holstein (the fifth of Queen Victoria's nine children). Within four years, with some additional building, mostly funded and furnished by Claude Montefiore himself, it would accommodate 160 children. Claude Montefiore also personally furnished and equipped the College library, and generously gave his own money repeatedly to offset the running costs of the Kindergarten and School. The Institute was fortunate indeed to have so committed a benefactor as Treasurer.

Sadly, on 21 May 1896 came the news of the death of Julia Salis-Schwabe the previous day in Naples at the age of 77. This was a profound shock to the FEI Committee. She had 'lived long enough to see one of the great dreams of her life become a reality', as the FEI Annual Report for 1896 stated. The funeral in Naples was conducted 'on a grand scale' (*Daily News,* 29 May). More than 100 carriages followed the coffin along a route crowded with teachers, pupils and other spectators. H.M.Consul attended, and the Empress Frederick and the Queen of Italy sent wreaths.

Challoner Street School (the 'low fee'd' practising school)

Miss Lawrence with a Challoner Street School class

In September 1896 the alumnae association, the Michaelis Guild, was established, by the first cohort of FEI students when the time had come for them to leave. (It was renamed 'Froebel Guild' 102 years later.) Its aims, as agreed at its first meeting on 18 September 1896, were: (i) to maintain the spirit of good fellowship amongst the old students; and (ii) to give help and sympathy on the practical carrying out of Froebel's principles. A member's badge was chosen (a green monogram, regarded as Froebel's colour, with a border of lilies, Froebel's symbolic flower), and in 1910 its regular newsletter, *Guild Notes,* came to be called *The Link,* a name which has lasted until 2001.

The 1890s, however, were also significant in marking an end to the first 'heroic' period of struggle for the Froebel movement in England. Bertha von Marenholtz-Bülow, the last major ideological link with Froebel, had died in 1893, and Luise Levin, Froebel's second wife, was to die in 1900. However, now, as the Victorian century was drawing to a close, a new, more prosaic, period of

struggle for survival was to ensue for the FEI. Naturally, there was a shortage of Practising Schools where trainees could find Froebelian methods in operation. The appeal for the free Practising School (now called, with unintended irony, the 'Popular Kindergarten') which was planned to occupy a second wing of the Institute had so far raised only £126. The Committee, therefore, in December 1896, proposed instead a Kindergarten and School for 'children of the smaller tradesmen and similar classes in Hammersmith and Kensington', to be 'under the control of the Committee and the direct supervision of the Principal, Madame Michaelis'. It would charge 'moderate' fees. But where would the capital come from?

Eventually, in November 1899 the Committee was able to report that it had rented a house in Challoner Street, five minutes' walk from the main Institute, for the establishment of what was now described as a 'low-fee'd' Kindergarten and School. It would be targeted at parents, 'especially among shopkeepers and clerks, who do not like to send their children to the National Elementary Schools, and yet cannot afford to pay the fees charged in private schools'. The first headmistress was Miss Violet Wallace, daughter of Professor Alfred Russell Wallace, socialist, explorer of the Amazon River and pioneer with Darwin of evolutionary theory. This School was to become known as 'Blue Froebel', and the Colet Gardens School as 'Green Froebel'.

In 1899 also four new classrooms were added to the Colet Gardens Demonstration School, paid for at a cost of £800 by Claude Montefiore, and were opened in the last month of the century by Sir George Kekewich,

Permanent Secretary at the Education Department. Mr Mather, Mr Montefiore, and General Schwabe all put their hands in their pockets to cover the deficit in the Annual Accounts of £66.

Some idea of educational conditions at the time is recorded by Christine Nance (Mrs Raymont), who was a student at FEI from 1897-99. Among her tutors was Miss E. Yeats, sister of the poet W.B. Yeats, who taught Painting at FEI for several years during and after the 1890s. She describes School Practice:

School Practice was usually in the Board Schools...some were appalling – dark buildings with windows too high for the children to look out...in some there were galleries of seats, tier upon tier, fifty or sixty children or even more...Most of the children were ragged and dirty and dressed in bits and pieces, some without shoes and stockings, and with knickers half way between knee and ankle...all spontaneous talk was suppressed until the children were afraid to talk. The natural result was that...they had to have special lessons in language...Lessons on the Postman were a great success, as we could make a game of

this and play at postman and posting letters...lessons on the Policeman were more difficult as most of the children regarded the 'copper' as an enemy from whom they must run...my object was to make them regard the policeman as a friend...The favoured few of us taught in the School attached to the College, or in the new School at Challoner Street. We thought the children in the FEI School far more difficult than the Challoner Street children.

Mme Michaelis with students

Esther Lawrence had deputised for Emilie Michaelis' absence for one term in autumn 1897, but at the end of the academic year in summer 1898 she resigned in order to visit Mme de Portugall at her Kindergarten and School in Naples. However, when in 1899, following a Report by one of Her Majesty's Inspectors, who had been invited to visit by the Committee, a new post of Mistress of Method was created, 'to supervise and assist students in their work, and to supplement by personal and individual attention their general training', Esther Lawrence returned to take up this post. In September 1901 she became Principal, on the retirement of Emilie Michaelis.

What was life like at the Froebel Educational Institute in its first years under Emilie Michaelis? The College offered training for 'those who wished to become educators of children in Kindergartens, Schools, and Private Families'. Two basic courses were offered, both including lectures, model lessons, and a course of practice under supervision:
• one for girls of 16 [soon raised to 17] (or suitable women above 20 who have no educational qualifications) in preparation for the Elementary Certificate of the National Froebel Union;
• another for girls of 17 [soon raised to 18] who hold the Elementary Certificate of the NFU, or a 'qualifying Certificate of sound general education', in preparation for the Higher Certificate of the NFU.

Though the Higher Certificate could take two years to complete, four terms was the standard length of study, and 'Fourth Term Highers' awards were an annual feature of College life, until about 1920. Fees were either eight or ten guineas for a twelve-week term. (A guinea was £1.05.) Dinner (= lunch) was provided for three guineas per term (60 meals). Hours of attendance were 9.30 to 12.30 and 2.00 to 4.30 every weekday.

The Kindergarten and School terms were thirteen weeks, 9.30 to 12.30, plus, for the School, 2.30 to 4.00 on three afternoons per week. Fees were between two guineas and four guineas per term, depending on age, and dinners were £2.10s per term. (10s was 50p.) There was a charge for materials of five shillings per term. Pupils ranged in age from under three to fifteen.

Numbers enrolled in the Kindergarten and School rose steadily to more than 90 by 1901, while those in the College remained fairly level at around 60-70, though in 1899 it was decided to reduce the numbers to below 50 owing to overcrowding.

The 'nearly-free' Kindergarten and School in Challoner Street recruited about 30 pupils per term in its first years of operation, all under eight years old, at a charge of ninepence (under 4p) per week – less than one-tenth of the *pro rata* charges at Colet Gardens. Numbers were less than had been hoped, and brought in little more than £50 per year, which did not even cover the rent, so the place was heavily subsidised, and prompted more calls for donations to FEI by the Executive Committee. It did, however, provide a suitable environment for teaching practice for training students – about twenty per term.

It is notable from the examination results in 1900-1902 that the pass rates in both Elementary and Higher Certificates at FEI were only about 70%. This was attributed by inspectors to the poor general education and literacy of a significant proportion of the intake – a problem noted in many of the training colleges at the time. In the 1890s at least half of women teachers in Board Schools (and at least one quarter of the men) had had no college training. The 'mutual instruction system' or monitorial system for producing teachers, developed by Andrew Bell and Joseph Lancaster during the previous century ('Give me twenty-four pupils today and I will give you twenty-four teachers tomorrow', claimed Bell), meant that fourteen-year-olds were teaching for five hours a day, with little knowledge or technique. This system changed after 1846 into pupil-teacher 'apprenticeships' with government salary. By the 1890s about six thousand boys and girls per year were completing these apprenticeships, but those that entered colleges found achieving adequate standards difficult, as, not unexpectedly, had their former pupils.

Unlike the non-Froebel training colleges, in which the main provision was for studying subjects to a more advanced level, together with some instruction in classroom organisation and in keeping discipline, the Froebel training emphasised at all stages a *philosophy of education* and the *wholeness* of the total educational process, based upon the *observation* of individual children. The philosophy enabled students to articulate long-term objectives, while the observation-based study of children prompted thoughts on ways to achieve them. The training was really directed at managing small groups of children in independent schools, rather than the very large classes of 50-70 in the board schools. The FEI emphasis throughout was more on process than outcome, which may also help to explain why there

seems to have been little or no preparation for examinations. There is a report that, one week before final examinations, when a student complained to Mme Michaelis that she had not even touched on the syllabus in her lectures, she gave what was acknowledged as her characteristic reply: 'I am making teachers, not examination puppets'.

Margaret McMillan (1860-1931)

During the Spring term 1899, Margaret McMillan, with five members of the Bradford School Board, visited FEI and wrote an account for the Bradford *Labour Echo*. They observed classes in the Model Kindergarten and School, and in the College. An excerpt in rhapsodic style (in the context, we must remember, of appalling conditions in Bradford) gives some impression of a day in the activity-based, holistic educational environment of FEI in its fifth year of existence:

Into the cool, quiet corridors of the bright spacious rooms the morning sun shone brightly. The parquetted floors, the wooden walls, the softly coloured ceiling were the framework of a tranquil and harmonised environment where the needs of the sub-conscious life were abundantly recognised. For the young child the tone is more than the word, the colour and the light is more than the lesson-book, the sights and sounds and contacts of the school are the influences that mould him, while to precept and moral he turns literally a DEAF EAR

Mme Michaelis and Miss Lawrence with graduating students, 1898

…Our first visit is paid to a class of small letter-writers. The little ones are not writing, however- they have a far more interesting employment! They are composing the letter – suggesting what shall be written, while the teacher selects and arranges, under collective surveillance! All the little faces are bright and animated…and when at last the letter is written and read to the class, it is pleasant to hear how smoothly it runs, to find one's own ideas expressed. And this exercise is fruitful. For through it language is taught – the troublesome word and letter are conquered.

…Here at last we come to a classroom where young teachers are receiving a lesson in botany, biology, zoology and also psychology – that is to say, the sciences concerning LIFE. They receive a special education, you see, and this is necessary. A young child is educated through Life – Life in all its forms, plant animal and human life. And it is only a teacher whose knowledge is wide and accurate who can select for him the vital facts which stimulate while they inform.

In 1900, the FEI gave up its voluntary status in order to become incorporated as a 'company, not for gain' under licence from the Board of Trade. This bestowed certain legal advantages, and its name was changed formally to the Incorporated Froebel Educational Institute (or IFEI), which it is still officially called today. A general meeting of members of the Association must be held once a year, which still takes place every December, though the Articles of Association were revised in 1921 to remove financial contribution as a requirement of membership.

Madame Michaelis tendered her resignation as Principal of FEI in March 1901, a month before her sixty-seventh birthday, though she accepted a seat on the Executive Committee. She was warmly remembered by her students and staff. One student wrote that 'her breadth of thought, wide outlook, and varied and interesting experiences gave to life and our work a zest and joy that nothing has ever taken away…you never went to her without being helped – comforted and strengthened in some way'. A student at FEI from 1894-97, Miss Evelyn Hope Wallace (who later became head of the Challoner Street School from 1902 until its closure in 1918), wrote of her that 'her presence was all-pervading…I can see her now, with her kind, loving eyes and wonderful smile beaming from under her beautiful black lace head-dress, speaking to us out of the depths of her rich experience'. Another student at FEI , Christine Nance (1897-99), wrote 'Academically her work may not have been much good, but she certainly did inspire me…it was a strange sight to see this little German lady, surrounded by a lot of young women wearing blouses and skirts reaching nearly to the ground, playing games of swinging, rolling or tossing these little balls…'. And her successor, Miss Esther Lawrence, who had been her deputy, wrote 'her sense of humour was extraordinarily keen, and she enjoyed a joke and a good story as much as anyone, and no College party was ever complete without Madame…the Institute and 'Madame' were synonymous'. She died not long after retirement, of 'a malignant disease', in December 1904.

In 1900, a young woman, Miss Rosalie Lulham, had been appointed tutor in Nature Study. (Along with Handwork, Nature Study was the subject most

fundamental to the kindergarten curriculum.) She became a distinguished zoologist and botanist and ardent field naturalist, whose textbooks became standard across the country, and she remained on the staff until her retirement in 1935. When well-equipped Zoology and Nature rooms had been built and equipped at Grove House, in the building now named after her, she was later fond of reminding people that 'in 1900 the entire equipment for the study of Nature consisted in one glass bell jar kept in a basement room in Colet Gardens'.

Claude Montefiore's book plate. He presented many hundreds of his books to the College library.

29

SIX

1901-1920: Through the Great War to Recognition by the Board of Education

J ANUARY 1901 had seen the death of Queen Victoria, which ended the longest reign of any British monarch. The poor survived in appalling social conditions, with perhaps 30% below the (low) poverty line. Factory legislation was now passed raising the age at which children could be legally employed from eleven to twelve (it became fourteen in 1920). This helped to protect children somewhat, but did not ameliorate the poverty problem.

Miss Lawrence in her study at Colet Gardens

Miss Esther Lawrence was immediately appointed as Principal to replace Mme Michaelis, a post which she was to hold with great distinction for a little over thirty years, and Miss A Yelland, who had been a mature student at FEI during 1895-96, replaced Miss Lawrence as headmistress of the Colet Gardens School, where she remained until her premature death in 1916.

Esther Lawrence had been born in the USA in 1862, into a cultured liberal Jewish family. They moved to England and settled in Hampstead while she was still a child. She had attended classes at Bedford College, London University in 1880-81, and then proceeded to train as a Froebel teacher at the Froebel Society Training College in Tavistock Place, gaining her Froebel Certificate in 1883, just before the college closed. She had then set up a private Kindergarten in Gower Street, before becoming head of the Preparatory Department of Chiswick High School, from which post she was appointed as Headmistress of the Colet Gardens School.

The new Principal of FEI was quite different in many ways from her predecessor. She was American/English rather than German, and this seemed symbolically to confirm the naturalisation of the kindergarten movement in Britain. She was Jewish, and this helped to ensure that the College remained non-denominational, unlike most teacher training colleges at the time. College assemblies were not based on any particular religious view – thus maintaining the Unitarian philosophy of Julia Salis-Schwabe and the interfaith perspective promoted by Claude Montefiore. College assemblies were held five days per week until 1939, and, rather than an act of worship, they were an expression of fellowship and affirmation of spiritual values. After 1929 they culminated in two minutes' communal silence, in order to encourage reflection and insight. Further, Miss Lawrence combined vision and practical determination to an unusual degree. Despite poor health (she had hearing problems, and later on kept a large amplifier box on her desk, which she took to High Table for dinner, and into which students would be expected to speak – when she turned it towards them!), she was a mentally strong woman, with enormous driving power harnessed to gentleness and a radiating serenity.

By now, the idealist mysticism of Froebel's writings was becoming very dated. The principles on which the 'gifts' and occupations, such as plaiting and paper-folding, were devised were seeming increasingly remote. Where adopted occasionally with large classes in Board Schools their rationale seemed quite recondite and abstruse. After sixty years and the passing of the first-generation Froebelians, a rethink of principles was overdue. This came significantly through the Mistress of Method at FEI, Maria Elizabeth Findlay (1855-1912), who had been appointed to FEI in 1898 and was also a member of the Council of the Froebel Society. She had previously been head of Stockton-on-Tees High School for Girls, and had subsequently studied psychology and then travelled to Canada and the USA, where she had visited schools influenced by John Dewey (1859-1952), whose book *School and Society* had been published in 1899. In an article in 1900, she argued strongly against those conservative kindergartners in the USA and England

who tried to maintain adherence to the mystical letter of Froebelian practice. Her position was soon supported by Elizabeth Murray, also a member of the Froebel Society Council. She was a lecturer at Maria Grey College, and argued at the Froebel Society Conference in 1901 that kindergarten games were valuable not for their symbolism but because of the social training they provided. She subsequently published an article in 1903 entitled 'That symmetrical paper folding and symmetrical work with the gifts are a waste of time for both students and children'. Essentially, the old-style Froebelians who had been running private kindergartens were being challenged by the new educational discourse emanating from the training colleges. There would be no return to the world and authority of 'the Master' as the new century progressed. New influences, including Dewey, Freud and Piaget would come irrevocably to inflect what was still known as 'Froebelianism'.

One of Miss Lawrence's first strategic acts as Principal in December 1901 was to apply to the University of London for recognition of FEI as a School of the University. In the previous year the University had adopted new Statutes, reconstituted itself into twenty-four Schools, and formally introduced the category of 'recognised teacher' in a number of affiliated institutions. (Prior to 1900 the University of London was an examining-only institution, with no involvement in teaching.) The reply from the Academic Registrar of the University, addressed to Arthur Symonds, the Secretary of FEI, in January 1902 was negative about School status, though willing for 'the University to influence its teaching etc.' if some FEI teachers were willing to apply for 'recognised' status. Miss Lawrence took no further

* N.B.—It is requested that two copies of this form be filled up.

THE UNIVERSITY OF LONDON.

Application for the Admission of:—

(a) *The Incorporated Froebel Educational Institute* (a) Here insert the name of the Institution.

as a School of the University.

December 1901

To the VICE-CHANCELLOR OF THE UNIVERSITY OF LONDON.

SIR,

I am directed by the Governing body of (a) *The Incorporated Froebel Educational Institute* to ask you to lay before the Senate of the University of London the application of (a) *the Incorporated Froebel Educational Institute* for admission as a School of the University.

(a) *The Incorporated F.E.I.* is a Public Educational Institution within the meaning of the Statutes of the University, and is situated at (b) *Talgarth Road, West Kensington* in the County of London. (b) Here insert the proper postal address of the Institution.

I append particulars of the constitution, financial position, and work of (a) *the Incorporated F.E.I.* and other information required under the Regulations for the admission of Public Educational Institutions as Schools of the University.

I have the honour to be,

(c) *E. E. Lawrence* (c) To be signed by the Principal or Acting Head of the Institution.

(d) *Vice President* (d) Here insert the proper designation of the person signing above.

Application for admission as a School of the University of London

UNIVERSITY OF LONDON,

SOUTH KENSINGTON, S.W.

January 28th, 1902.

Dear Sir,

In further reference to your letter of the 11th inst, I am now able to say that I have seen Sir Edward Busk, and he agrees with me in thinking that there is no machinery by which the Froebel Institute could be "recognised" as a Training ~~Institute~~ College of the University. He fancies you may have possibly misunderstood some remark of his. What he desired to suggest was that it would be possible for the Institute to come into connection with the University, and for the University to influence its teaching etc. if some of its Teachers were recognised by the University in connection with ~~your~~ their work at the Institute. It is not, however, possible for the University to recognise the Institute as a whole.

Yours faithfully,

H. Frank Heath

Academic Registrar.

A. G. Symonds, Esq,
The Incorporated Froebel Educational Institute,
Talgarth Road,
West Kensington,
W.

The reply. Later in the same year the London County Council, about to become a 'Local Education Authority' under the terms of the 1902 Act, founded the London Day Training College, which 30 years later became the University of London Institute of Education and subsequently a School of the University action on this offer (though some London training colleges did, including Maria Grey). However, it is not without irony that in the same year, 1902, the London County Council set up the 'London Day Training College' in Clare Market (behind the current LSE), which in 1932 became the University of London Institute of Education, the body which was within fifty years to oversee all teacher education in London.

On the national scene, a new Education Act was passed by the Conservative government in 1902 (the 'Balfour' Act), which abolished all 2586 School Boards, and placed the board schools under newly formed Local Education Authorities, who were empowered to establish secondary and technical schools. It was to be a 'national system, locally administered', the national controlling body being the Board of Education, which had been established three years earlier. In Britain in 1900, only one child in 70 was receiving any secondary education at all, and in City of London offices thousands of well-educated German clerks were carrying on the work of commerce. The developing imperial economy needed a white-collar work force, but the education system was failing to provide one, by comparison with Germany.

The Act also decreed that rate aid should go to all Voluntary Schools, including denominational schools, and this led to violent protests and 'passive resistance' (the phrase came into the language because of this issue) by non-conformists, who objected to paying rates in support of denominational schools. The argument became a major election issue in 1905, when the Conservative government was overthrown and a Liberal government returned. Education was now a hot issue in the public mind, though much of the emphasis was moving towards the need for secondary provision. Nevertheless during these years FEI was becoming increasingly widely known, and was attracting visitors almost daily from all over the world to its College, its demonstration Kindergarten and School at Colet Gardens, and its practising Kindergarten in Challoner Street nearby. It was confirming an international reputation that would last throughout the twentieth century.

In the spring of 1902, The FEI Committee applied for recognition as 'a place for the purpose of training secondary teachers' under the new legislation, and, as a result, there was a full inspection of FEI by the Board of Education later that year, in November.

The Inspection Report states that 'the financial position of the undertaking is far from satisfactory and would be very serious indeed, if it were not for the generosity of friends who have contributed specially from time to time towards reduction of deficits'. The three years to September 1902 carried an accumulated deficit of £1,041, of which £650 was covered by an advance from the Treasurer (Claude Montefiore). In the light of this severe financial situation, the Report comments that 'it will probably be thought that the salaries both of the Principal of the Institute and of the Headmistress of Colet Gardens School (£200 and £130 a year respectively) should be increased', and also that 'the fees in the Training College, ranging from £8.8s to £10.10s a term, are higher than those charged at some similar institutions'. It went on to recommend 'the possible sources of [financial] assistance are two – grants from the County Council or other local authority, and aid from endowment'.

Some further points from the Report were:
- the Principal appears to possess good organising ability, and carries out her duties efficiently;
- the Principal does not teach in the Schools…the time she spends in teaching in the Training College varies; during the last term it was four hours weekly…in addition to this, she acts as "tutor" to the students, seeing the students individually about their work;
- the qualifications of the staff are very satisfactory…all the members of the permanent staff possess recognized diplomas or certificates of a general education; and all are "trained" teachers holding certificates of either the National Froebel Union, or the Cambridge Teachers' Syndicate…and only four have had less than four years' experience in teaching;
- the Training Department provides a course of study which will fit the students for their professional work; it accordingly does not undertake their general education…but instruction in Drawing, Mathematics, and Natural Science is wisely added so as to add to the students' knowledge and to show them how to use it for teaching purposes;
- 16 hours a week [are] given to the theoretical work, and about three mornings a week to the practical work;
- *Theoretical work:* The syllabus of the work is excellent;
- *Practical work:* All this is excellent;

- *Actual teaching under supervision:* The teaching work is on the whole adequate, especially as most of the students spend two years at the Institute, and thus get at least 180 hours' teaching, but the resources of the College in this respect must, with the present number of 64 students, have pretty nearly reached their limit;
- *Natural Science:* It is unfortunate that more practical work is not done;
- *Mathematics*: As careful instruction in number and form is a necessary part of Froebelian practice…it is satisfactory to find that it is in such capable hands;
- *Drawing*: The Scheme of study is sound…but more time should be allotted to Drawing on the Blackboard;
- *Teaching in the Training College*: The instruction as a

Blackboard Drawing was an essential part of the Froebel Certificate

Kindergarten in Mysore, 1907. Froebel graduates spread to all parts of the world from the early days of FEI

whole is given excellently…at the discussion which one of the Inspectors attended, in his opinion the teacher did too much work, and there was an absence of free discussion.

An insight into Colet Gardens School may be gained from the Inspectors' observation that 'the discipline of the children is good though a great deal of freedom is allowed. It might, however, be suggested that the children should be taught to refrain from excessive gesticulation in class'. And, in relation to geography, 'the topics selected for last term were World Pictures of England, Greece, India, China, South Africa, Egypt, Canada, South America, Australia. These countries are far removed from the mental grasp of the children of the average age of $7^1/_2$. It would be better to take subjects nearer home.' The eternally unimaginative dead hand of the Inspector.

The Report concluded that 'the Institution is well organized and efficiently managed and fulfils its present

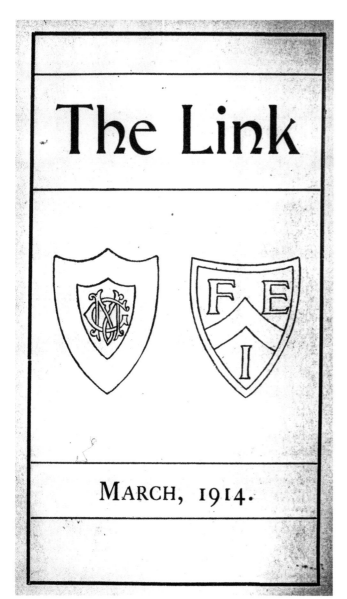

Cover of an early edition of *The Link,* showing the Michaelis Guild crest and an early FEI crest

purpose admirably', but advised that to extend its brief to the training of secondary teachers would entail many new problems: finance, space, availability of practising schools, and entry qualifications of students. Nevertheless, it was 'not an absolutely impossible task'. In the event, the College did not move into secondary training, despite the declaration in the first *Prospectus* of 1892. Finances were an ever-present concern, with both schools losing money, and depending on the fund-raising efforts of students.

The College continued to consolidate its position, reputation and influence in the years up to and including World War One. In this heyday of Empire, trained students from FEI were travelling to many parts of the world. In the 1915 edition (no.6) of *The Link*, the alumnae magazine founded in 1910 and still published in 2001, is a 7-page article, under the heading 'Our Members in Other Lands', consisting of messages and news from former students in Canada, Africa, Australia, New Zealand, India, Ceylon, as well as China, the USA, and many parts of Europe. By 1923, 'Round the World with our Members' took up 28 pages of the magazine, recording the work of scores of former students all over the world.

Meanwhile, in London in 1908 and 1912, Miss Lawrence herself financed the establishment of two free kindergartens on behalf of FEI, in Notting Hill and St Pancras. They survived until after World War Two, and were also supported by funds raised by the Michaelis Guild (the alumnae association), and staffed mainly by former students. One colleague later recalled the motivation for Miss Lawrence's determination to set up these schools:

LEFT 1915

Graduating class of 1915 on the front steps at Colet Gardens

On our bus ride home from Colet Gardens we used to pass through one of the most sordid streets of London lodging houses. Half-naked babies crawled up and down the filthy doorsteps, pale-faced, ragged children swarmed on the pavement, or dodged in and out of the traffic. Miss Lawrence would speak with passion of the needs of childhood, of the right of all children, rich and poor, to share the good things of life – green fields to run on, trees to climb, contact with the clean earth, pure air to breathe. Such were the heritage of childhood, and it was for us to struggle to achieve this end.

It is also of note that in December 1912 Miss Lawrence gave an address to the Froebel Society comparing the work in these free kindergartens with that in the Montessori Children's Houses in Italy. Some Froebelians resented Mme Montessori's criticism of Froebel's methods. Miss Lawrence, however, welcomed the Montessori 'experiments', and had been one of the first to present Montessori apparatus to British teachers. She was, however, aware of the limitations of a 'technique' that had no supporting philosophy to generate imagination and 'unity', and argued that, without the genius and understanding of Mme Montessori herself, children soon tired of the 'method'.

The coming of the 1914-18 war brought many pressures and forced serious decisions on FEI. Miss Yelland, the much loved and respected headmistress of the Demonstration School who had been appointed when Miss Lawrence became Principal of FEI in 1901, had died unexpectedly in April 1916 at the age of 50. In 1917, Sir William Mather retired through ill-health from the Chairmanship of FEI (being replaced in the role by Claude Montefiore), and was to die three years later, at the age of 82, having been a loyal and generous supporter of the Institute since its inception.

It was easy at this time to get depressed, as the War, after Gallipoli and the Battle of the Somme, seemed to get bogged down in futility, with hundreds of thousands of British losses. Everyone knew someone who had not returned from the front. There was strong anti-German feeling and there were even anti-German riots in places. The royal family changed their dynastic name from Saxe-Coburg (inherited through the late Prince Albert) to Windsor in 1917, in the same year and for the same

Colet Gardens: playing at Native Americans

reason that the Battenberg family changed their name to Mountbatten: to avoid becoming the focus of the strong anti-German feeling. The Froebel name was not abandoned, however, and Miss Lawrence, together with the FEI Governing Body, retained a positive outlook. In fact, Miss Lawrence proposed a programme of expansion.

The war was highlighting a massive demand for nursery schools, as fathers were fighting at the front, and mothers were going out to work on the land, in munitions factories, as bus-drivers, etc. in support of the war effort. In 1917, the year of the Bolshevik Revolution and the year of the entry of the USA into the War, the Executive Committee of FEI recognised and responded to the need for development and for more accommodation for the Institute. Launching an appeal (which proved unsuccessful) for £8,000 for purchase of a 58-year lease on studios in Talgarth Road, they produced an upbeat statement, responding in part to statements by the national Education Reform Council:

Since the War began the fundamental principles of education for which the Institute was founded twenty-five years ago have become more generally recognised and advocated. The Committee earnestly desire that the Institute should not only keep abreast of the important development now taking place in the educational worlds at large, but should itself continue to take an active part in solving the educational problems which are before the country at the present time.

Some pupils at the School around this time were subsequently to become famous. The humourist Arthur Marshall was at Colet Gardens from 1916-18, and in later life recalled:

I think there was a Miss Bain who was mad keen on Red Indians and with whom we dressed up and crept into wigwams…Some time ago I exchanged letters with Imogen Holst, and I think we found that we had just overlapped at the school.

It was at these wartime lunches that I formed a deep dislike of lentils. I am not speaking of lentil soup…but of lentils nature, plain and untampered with as they left their Maker…Rightly informed by those in authority that our food, lentils especially, came to us, very bravely brought, over the seas, we sang every morning the same hymn 'Eternal Father Strong to Save' and intended to help those in peril on the sea. One sang as loudly as possible, feeling that it might help more towards the safety of the vital cargoes…The combination of the foreign words 'kindergarten' and 'Froebel' convinced one of my school friends that all the schoolmistresses were German spies…

A blindfold game at an indoor class at Colet Gardens Demonstration School

Student tennis at Colet Gardens

Colet Gardens, 1900s. Outdoor exercises were considered very important

Student gardening: cultivating an awareness of the four seasons was an important part of Froebelian training

My two years there were an enchanted time. I remember no punishments, no rows, no squabbles. We seldom sat at benches or desks. Our schoolmistresses never frowned at us. In this happy and harmonious paradise we sang, we painted, we made cardboard models, we stuck chestnut buds in jam jars, we acted Hiawatha, we became Knights with shields and swords, we kept animals. We skipped on fine days and bowled hoops. There were puppets and a water-tank and a revolving summerhouse and a sandpit. There was a library (somewhere along the way I learnt to read) and we were encouraged into it. One absorbed a great deal and almost without realising it. The building itself lacked beauty but we hurried to it in the morning with joy and left it at tea-time with regret.

At this time both College and School were overcrowded: the College had about 90 students, while the Kindergarten and School had expanded to take 200 children aged between three and fourteen. Fees at the College and at the Demonstration Kindergarten and School were still virtually unchanged since inception. The Institute was now self-supporting for the first time, though the losses at Challoner Street were a drain on any potential surplus. The FEI Executive wanted the Institute to become 'an increasingly important research and experimental centre in the educational development of the nation', and to attract more postgraduate students. It regretted that there was no residential facility for students (who were being boarded in various small houses in the neighbourhood). Perhaps because wartime was not a propitious time to appeal for financial aid, the appeal came to nothing.

But implicit in the appeal were serious questions for FEI to address: what was the mission of FEI? Was it to produce more free schools for the poor on a shoestring? or was it to take the lead in research and development of Froebelian principles? How important was a collegiate environment for the growth and development of Froebelian teachers? It was known that a new Education Act was impending. How could FEI, in its current overcrowded premises and delicate financial situation, play a proper role in any new national developments?

One answer was given at that start of 1918 with the closure of Challoner Street Kindergarten and School. It could not continue being subsidised by FEI, despite having about 100 children on roll, and despite much-increased fees of between three and nine guineas per term. (Its joint headmistresses, Miss Hope Wallace and Miss Malin – known affectionately as 'Mutt and Jeff' because one was tall and thin and the other short and plump – went on to open a school of their own in Queen's Gate, South Kensington, which they called 'Challoner', in memory of the FEI school). The closure was significant. It affirmed that the true function of FEI was pedagogic development, not spreading a fixed idea by opening charity nurseries. It committed itself implicitly, under Miss Lawrence's wise direction, to spreading change nationally and interactively with government through providing the best training for committed teachers. Its two-and-a-third-year training programme would shortly be increased to three years.

Miss Lawrence, writing in spring 1918, posed the following questions:

Has the FEI accomplished its allotted task, or has it failed in its endeavours? And if the answer is in the affirmative in either case, is one justified in adding links to the chain, is one justified in "carrying on"?

Summoning all her visionary determination, qualities desperately needed at this time, and perhaps echoing those voices and values that would lead to the establishment of the League of Nations the following year, she answers:

We may say that the allotted task of a Froebelian institution is infinite, and can therefore never be "accomplished". But just because the issues are immense, and are in many respects above us, we feel inspired to go on and on. The further we progress, notwithstanding innumerable halts and stumbles, the more fully conscious we become of the work and of its many and diverse details. And if we realize – and the war has probably helped us to realize – that the work of teachers, both in and out of the FEI, is as great and important as any work in all the world, we shall forge ahead and tackle it with renewed insight and courage. In the children of today lies the hope of the future. Work with and for children is in itself, and notwithstanding its difficulties, full of satisfaction and joy…Let us press forward and realize, through our children, some of the ideals for which the world is striving.

1918 also saw the passing of the Education Act (the 'Fisher' Act), which made schooling compulsory up to the age of 14, abolished all fees in elementary schools, and increased the powers of LEAs. The Act aimed to establish 'a national system of public education available for all persons capable of profiting thereby', and so for the first time England and Wales had a free and compulsory (to age 14) system of state education. LEAs were shortly afterwards empowered to finance the provision of nursery schools (though not many did), and in 1921 the Burnham Committee was set up to determine national rates of pay for teachers.

The end of the War was initially a cause for ecstatic celebration. Hilda Feather (Mrs Chapman), who was a student at FEI from 1916-19 recalls:

I remember walking out into the Entrance Hall and our secretary, Miss Kerr – utterly controlled and rather prim to the superficial eye – rushing out of her office and seizing me with both hands as she swung me round in a crazy circle, tears splashing down her face as she gasped "It's over! It's over! The war is over!" College emptied. Everyone rushed out to climb on bus stops and go to join the crowds in Trafalgar Square.

In 1920 FEI was formally 'recognised' by the Board of Education, and as a consequence the length of the standard training course was increased to three years – one year longer than non-Froebelian training colleges. Recognition meant that students could receive grants towards tuition for years two and three. This new three-year course was recognised by the Teachers Registration Council. In addition, as a further consequence and mark of its growing self-reliance, the College in 1921 for the first time set its own internal examination papers, which were externally examined by the NFU, so that students could receive the Froebel Teacher's Certificate, no longer divided into 'elementary' and 'higher'. This was the end

The Gliddon Road Hostel

of the two-year-plus-one-term training which had existed hitherto.

For a few months in 1921, Marie ('Mimi') Michaelis, the daughter of Emilie Michaelis, who had attended Girton College Cambridge in the 1890s, and subsequently had been a tutor at Maria Grey College, was welcomed as Vice-Principal of the College. However, she left within the year to study auto-suggestion and the art of healing. She kept in touch with the College, writing regular letters on the benefits of auto-suggestion (or, positive thinking), and returned to visit the College many times, her last visit being in 1958 when she opened the Michaelis Hall, named in honour of her mother.

In the same year, 1921, a hostel for students was opened in Gliddon Road, off Talgarth Road, very close to Colet Gardens, catering for 40 students. Most of the rooms slept two, three or four students, and were divided up by curtains. There were also study rooms, a drawing room, and a dining room.

The College in 1920 had 173 students on roll, and the School had 260. Despite the new hostel, it could hardly be called a residential college, the creation of which was Miss Lawrence's ambition. The ancient universities and many training colleges were residential, and it was thought that furthering the College's mission could be especially enhanced by the moral support which communal residence could give. Miss Lawrence, ever resourceful and foresightful, records in March 1921:

The College has quite outgrown its premises, and diligent search is being made for a suitable "out-size" building in which our enlarged family may live, by night as well as by day, for we hope the College may become residential…Many have been the visits of inspection made by members of the Committee and Staff to possible properties round about London…Picnics en route *have given the searchers strength to face tumble-down hospitals, hotels and hydros, which are "to be let or sold". Mr Montefiore has found coffee in a thermos a great inducement to take part in the house-hunting expeditions, and his presence has never failed to cheer the other searchers…Nothing is yet settled, but a house in large grounds on the top of a hill in the south of London seems to hold the field as we go to press* [i.e. March 1921]. *However, it may not hold the field for long…Unfortunately, much money has to be found as well as house and grounds, and many of us are prepared to beg from door to door.*

1921-1931: New Premises – Grove House, Roehampton

I N fact the house on a hill was Grove House, the present home of the College. Close contenders were houses in Ham Common and in Norwood, but Grove House was the final decision. At that time Roehampton was an exclusive residential area, located to the west of Putney and with many fine 18th-century mansions. Grove House was a Georgian building dating from about 1790. During the Great War it had been used by the Royal Flying Corps (predecessor of the RAF), and was empty, riddled with dry rot and otherwise severely neglected. 'A god-forsaken spot', muttered Mr Montefiore when he first saw it. The thistles and weeds on the lawn were so high that the lake was not visible from the terrace. Nevertheless, in August 1921 he

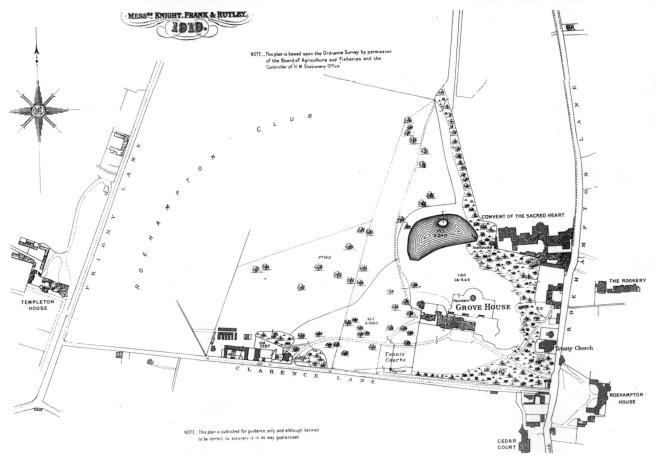

Plan of Grove House estate in 1919, provided to FEI by the estate agents

Froebel Educational Institute, Grove House, Roehampton Lane. Front View.

Front of Grove House, 1920s. Note the unextended single-storey Dining Room, later to become known as the Portrait Room.

purchased the freehold with 33 acres for FEI, for £29,750. (Following the decline in value of the pound after the War, this was worth about 24 times the equivalent sum today, though of course the value of land in London has risen dramatically since then.)

During that summer of 1921 a gang of Canadian lumberjacks cleared the trees on the land leading down to the lake, and within four weeks before the end of September 40 temporary single-storey student bedrooms, to house 80 students, were built, together with three lecture rooms. These became known as the 'bungies'

GROVE HOUSE. ROEHAMPTON. from the Air.

Grove House from the air, showing the temporary bungalow residences

acquired to accommodate a similar number of students. The Demonstration School in Colet Gardens overflowed into the former college rooms to accommodate its 260 children aged 3-14. Though $2^1/_2$ miles away, it was still used regularly by second- and third-year students at Grove House for observation and practice. As one former student commented, 'the conductors and passengers on the 73 bus soon got used to seeing girls boarding the bus in Roehampton Lane, armed with jam jars full of tadpoles, branches of trees, flowers, fishing nets and live rabbits to be used on teaching practices'.

[bungalows], and one resident was later to comment, 'they were noisy, restless places…you had your friends around you and there was no need to leave your room to converse with those next door or over the passage'.

Grove House took longer to prepare, as gas, electricity, heating and kitchens had to be installed or renovated. Nevertheless the College, with 115 resident students and 70 day students, commenced work in its exciting new premises in January 1922. In February, Queen Mary visited the College, was given a tour of the grounds in Mr Montefiore's car, observed some teaching, and had tea in the Principal's panelled office on the ground floor.

The recently acquired hostel in Gliddon Road, though temporarily closed, was reopened in September 1922 and was retained until November 1929, when Templeton, an eighteenth-century house near to Grove House, was

The *Prospectus* for the new three-year training programme outlined the following syllabus:

The following subjects are included in the course, and their application to the education of children is specially studied:
1. *Literature, Geography, History*
2. *Nature Knowledge (Botany and Zoology)*
3. *Elements of Mathematics*
4. *Hygiene*
5. *Singing and Theory of Music*
6. *Handwork (Drawing, Painting, Carpentry, Clay-modelling, Weaving, Toy-making, etc.*
7. *Eurhythmics, Games, and other Physical Exercises*
8. *Psychology, with special Study of Child Nature and Development*
9. *History of Education, with special application to Social and Civic Developments.*

Compared with the earlier syllabus, the main difference is the omission of explicit reference to Froebel's Principles, his two books, or to the Kindergarten Gifts and Occupations. These would have come in to the curriculum under items 6 and 9, but perhaps the omission was because the College was modernising its approach to professional training.

In 1922 fees were raised by £3.3s, to £12.12s per term for year one and £15.15 for years two and three, but the separately payable £6.6s examination fee (which went to the NFU) was abolished, as the examinations were now being internally set and marked. Students were now eligible for partial grant funding from the Board of Education, up to a maximum of £20 p.a. for tuition and £28 for residence for years two and three only. Year One was still fully self-financed, and this was an implicit selection criterion for students, as their families would need to have access to sufficient capital to afford this unsupported expenditure. The financial records show that the Board of Education grants never amounted to more than 20-25% of total tuition and residence income. Residence cost 33 guineas per term, with five dinners and teas per week costing £4.4s per term in addition.

Although not foreseen at the time, the economic slump of 1922, the General Strike of 1926 and the economic crisis and great depression of 1931 were to produce massive economic turbulence in all sections of society, to which FEI would not be immune.

As a result of the purchase of Grove House, FEI once again had immense debts, and was able to survive only because of the amazing generosity of Claude Montefiore

The total cost of moving to Grove House was not merely the nearly £30,000 basic cost (Miss Lawrence herself loaned £5,000), but also legal costs and costs of refurbishment and new teaching buildings, making a total indebtedness of FEI within two years of £65,000. In a statement of 20 November, 1921, Mr Montefiore asked merely 'for the return of capital as soon as is convenient and feasible', without interest. The Board of Education required that ownership should not reside with a private individual, as FEI would be repaying loans partly with

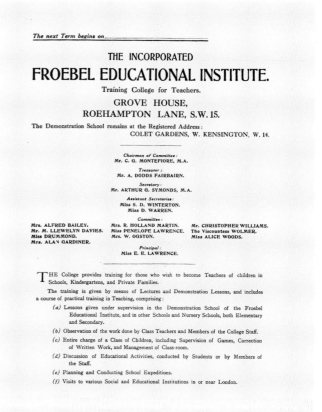

The first (1922) Prospectus for the new address

FEI staff in 1925, with Claude Montefiore and 'Bobby', with Miss Lawrence on his right, and Miss Sharp and then Miss Lulham on his left

education and supervision before that age. The government has decided (and I think rightly decided) to adopt the latter alternative'. In 1925 the Circular was published which virtually eliminated all under-fives from state education by forcing LEAs to make savage cuts in expenditure in this sector. The next year, the year of the General Strike, the national economy was so dire and unemployment so high that teachers had massive salary cuts of up to 50% or even lost their jobs altogether. It was also the case that untrained graduate teachers were on a scale recommended by the Burnham Committee of £275-£440, whereas three-year trained teachers were on a scale of £210-£360 – and many were getting less than that. (Multiply by 32 for today's approximate value.) This was not a good time economically for expanding the recruitment and training of teachers.

Government grants, so ownership was transferred to FEI. By 1925, the College had raised only £3,574 to offset this sum. Eventually the loan unobtrusively became a gift.

In early 1922, H.A.L Fisher, who was still President of the Board of Education, under pressure from the Geddes Economy Committee to make cuts in public spending, proposed that infant schools did not need trained staff, other than the head teacher and perhaps an assistant, and that they could make do, as during the War, with uncertificated young women. Claude Montefiore protested on behalf of the Froebel Society, but Herbert Fisher replied that 'the alternatives before us were either the exclusion of children from school until they reach the age of six, or a reduction in the cost of their

In this context of uncertainty about the future, FEI was in the middle of an extensive programme of building on the Grove House estate. The first building, ready in 1923, was a single-storey building, now called Lulham (after Rosalie Lulham, the long-serving Nature Study tutor), which comprised an assembly hall, zoology and botany rooms, handwork rooms, and space for eurhythmics.

In 1925-26 the curriculum came under close scrutiny. Miss Lawrence posed the question: 'Ought we to aim at scholarly work in a few subjects, or at a bird's eye view of the whole?' The first year programme was mainly academic, and was being criticised by students as 'too much like school work'. They wanted to get on with the practical and professional work from the start. In 1928 Miss Lawrence was advocating a change on these lines, but reported that 'the NFU gives very little liberty in this respect'. She noted that although some parents were urging students to attend University Colleges, many preferred to attend Froebel Colleges, because they wanted to begin on practical and professional work as soon as possible. However, the NFU remained permanently inflexible on this point, refusing to allow school experience until the very end of Year One, on the principle, apparently, that students must *know* something before they can teach it. Miss Lawrence posed the question as to whether the curriculum in schools was too narrow and scholastic, and that this was alienating students from academic study.

The NFU was at the peak of its power and prestige at this time, though, of course, it did not know it. In 1929 universities had taken over from the Board of Education responsibility for the examination of students in training colleges for the purpose of their recognition as certificated teachers. Each university and its associated colleges had formed a Joint Board which appointed external examiners (mostly from the staff of the university), discussed syllabuses, and certified results to the Board of Education. The National Froebel Union was honoured by being recognised as 'equivalent' to the Joint Boards, in that its own Certificates were recognised as conferring Qualified Teacher status in the colleges offering an NFU approved Froebel training. FEI was

therefore not a member of a university-based Joint Board at this time.

The excitement of the College's move from Colet Gardens to Grove House was captured by a student (Dorothy Venour) for whom the move took place at the start of her third year. She was later to become Warden and Principal of the 'offspring' college at Offley Place in Hertfordshire after World War Two. She writes, reflecting ten years later on the move to Grove House:

> Then we had little more than the space of a hard tennis court, and a strip of garden for small plots, which could be called "grounds"…now we have nine tennis courts, two netball pitches, and three hockey fields, besides all the grassy pleasances and shady trees. Then we were delighted with our little concrete pond a few feet in diameter. Now we have a lake several hundred yards across [sic], and a lily pond with a fountain. Then the First Years had all their lectures in

Froebel Educational Institute, Grove House, Roehampton Lane. Library.
The original Library at Grove House, now called the Adam Room

one room…now First years find it a real convenience to have a bicycle for getting from one building to another for different lectures…

Margaret Isherwood, a lecturer in Psychology from 1921-27, recalls:

[Miss Lawrence] apologised for the general confusion of those early days of the removal when nothing was really ready for students or staff…When the first excitement was over and the cold weather came, the students, not unnaturally, had some grumbling to do. "You ask for another blanket because you're cold at night, and you're told 'Yes, but look at the beautiful view'."

Mr Montefiore was a frequent visitor in those days, and his visits were a source of delight to us all. He and Miss Lawrence could be very entertaining when they got on the platform together at the after-lunch assemblies we had at 2.00 p.m. He had a great gift of humour and would sometimes have the whole assembly rocking with laughter.

The experience which was by common consent the very worst for students up to and including the 1930s was the Criticism lesson, known as the 'Crit' lesson. This was where a student would teach a class in front of the Psychology lecturer, the Mistress of Method, the class teacher, and the entire year-group of students for that age-phase, all of whom would afterwards report on what they had observed.

One pupil at the Colet Gardens School at this period (1924-32) was Iris Murdoch, the novelist. She later recalled:

My days at the Froebel were entirely happy ones…being "taught" at that school was both rigorous and painless…my pictures of those schooldays are of light, of freedom and happiness, the great greedy pleasures of learning, the calm kindly authority of teachers, the gentle friendliness of children. Those were the days of Miss Bain, our magisterial and warmhearted headmistress, and of "Knights and Ladies", now a legend. "Knights and Ladies" involved a segregation, not into "houses" but into "households" whereby the older children responsibly looked after "their own" younger children. Thus titles came into my life innocuously early on. This omnipresent form of "chivalry" was more than a game, though a great deal of theatre and delightful dressing-up was involved. A spirit of courtesy, of dignity, of standards, of care for others was painlessly induced.

We had excellent teachers…I especially remember Miss Burdett who taught me Latin…Another thing I learnt at the Froebel was cricket…I was also taught the basis for handwriting called "script", which inculcates respect for individual letters. The first model sentence I wrote, practising that lovely hand which has remained with me ever since, was "The snowdrop hangs down her lovely head. Why?" *Why indeed! A thought-provoking question, a good introduction to a world which is full of mysteries.*

Meanwhile, building and purchases continued – all at Mr Montefiore's expense. A residence block, New Court, was opened in 1926. In 1927, the whole of Grove house and the other original buildings were rewired, and the Dining Room (now the Portrait Room) was extended,

The Dining Room before enlargement

Templeton in 1929

continue to live in hopes of having an Art Room before long', reported Miss Lawrence to the Michaelis Guild. In fact, a new and stylish art and craft building was opened in 1929, and in the same year a nearby eighteenth-century house with four acres, Templeton in Priory Lane, was purchased, increasing the residential capacity of the Roehampton campus considerably.

Templeton had briefly been the home of Winston Churchill and his wife Clementine in 1919, as it was then owned by his cousin, Freddie Guest, who was a grandson of the seventh Duke of Marlborough and an MP from 1910 to 1929. Miss Lawrence subsidised the purchase price of £14,000 with a loan of £10,000. A new road had been cut behind Templeton and called 'Templeton Road', which was made up in 1934 and is now known as Roehampton Gate.

Edith Buswell, the first Warden of Templeton recalls:

We moved up to Templeton from West Kensington during a half-term in November 1929. The move should have been in the summer holidays, then suddenly the LCC [London County Council] came down on us and ordered teak floors to be put along the corridors and several inches of asbestos underneath...however we managed...after West Kensington it was all so spotlessly clean! The stables for the Polo Ground joined the courtyard at Templeton, and the ponies were a great attraction to the students, especially to those who were used to riding at home. When Mr Trent suggested they should exercise the ponies they were very excited.

with twelve bedrooms and bathroom facilities built overhead. In 1928 a small row of study bedrooms was built near the pigsties (pigs had been introduced to use up kitchen waste profitably), which was known then as the Piggeries, now as Redford House Nursery. 'If we are not faced with new and unexpected expenses, and if our numbers remain high, Mr Montefiore thinks we may

In 1928 there were 252 students enrolled on the three-year course, and the figure remained at or near this level for several years, until World War II. All these students needed more opportunity to observe children at close quarters, and so another Demonstration School, in addition to the one remaining in Colet Gardens, was added to the Grove House estate. A building at the west end of the campus which had originally been built as an electricity substation, and which had been used for Nature Study (it was near the greenhouses and kitchen garden), was reconditioned and extended to include a further room and cloakrooms in 1928, and further extended in 1930, in order to provide accommodation for a fee-paying school for 60 children. It was called Grove House School, and stayed open until September 1939. Miss Lawrence donated a 12-seater bus to the school, so that children could be transported safely from and to their homes, and many College staff taught there. The bus was painted green and white, which by now had become the FEI colours (green because it was thought to be Froebel's favourite colour, being the colour of nature and growth).

Student Reminiscences from the 1920s

Dinner at High Table was the occasional dreaded event. Two students each night, one seated beside, one opposite Miss Lawrence. She had a little black hearing aid box. When this was turned to face you, you were expected to make conversation. Miss Lawrence, when you had some personal contact, was a dear, though very autocratic, and very caring about students.
I can remember all my year students setting off for teaching practice on bikes, during the general strike, complete with rolls of pictures, various teaching aids and, of course, the pounding jar. It was my ambition to get across Hammersmith Broadway without dismounting – which I did occasionally! (C.C. 1924-27)

I remember having elocution lessons with a teacher who came in from outside the college. She insisted that our voices must have life and variation. I'll never forget reciting: 'By the waters of Babylon there we sat down and oo – ept'!
Although going to FEI after University was a bit like going to boarding school, I enjoyed my time there and certainly have found it a most valuable training. Frequently during the years I taught, Inspectors would come along with an exciting 'new' approach to teaching – but I had been doing it for years! That was the Froebel method. This especially applied to learning through experience (having a shop, making bread and butter etc.). (J.P. 1928-30)

Did you ever get 'late leave' until 11.15 p.m., then walk up Roehampton Lane alone? (Forbidden). Then as the door was opened, shout to your imaginary escort, "Goodnight and thank you for a lovely evening"? (M.S. 1928-31)

EIGHT

1932-1939: The Thirties

MISS Lawrence had retired at the end of 1931, from a college well-established and flourishing, and having apparently convinced a major Committee of the Board of Education itself of the rightness of its principles and methods. The Report, *Infant and Nursery Schools,* published by the Board in 1933, was the third part of a composite Report published between 1926 and 1933 on the organisation, objective and curriculum of schools in England and Wales. Known as the Hadow Report, after its Chairman, it was an endorsement of Froebelian principles. Froebel is identified on page one as 'the first great educator on the Continent who endeavoured to provide a coherent scheme of infant education based on the nature of the child'. The Report deplores the fact that Froebel's gifts and occupations were often taught mechanically in large classes, or treated as 'mere toys or amusing pastimes'. It rejects traditional 'subjects' presented as 'lessons to be mastered', and proposes instead 'methods which take as the starting point...the experience, the curiosity, and the awakening powers and interests of the children themselves'. The curriculum was to be thought of 'in terms of activity and experience', and the aim should be 'to develop in a child the fundamental human powers and to awaken him to the fundamental interests of civilized life so far as these powers and interests lie within the compass of childhood'. Influenced by the young Professor Cyril Burt (who, after his death in 1971, was to become notorious for his research on IQ testing), the Report quotes him as arguing that 'there should be little or no formal instruction before the age of six at the very earliest'. It identifies 'Froebel's master principle, and his enduring contribution to educational theory' as the following, which 'thoughtful teachers' had deduced: 'the

Miss Lawrence, holding her hearing aid, with Miss Jebb on the Grove House Terrace, 1933

mechanical use of the Froebel gift [...] ... 1889 ... [school] ... 1930 with every child copying the teacher rather than engaging in creative play

A Nature Knowledge class with Miss Lulham at the back, 1930s

younger cousin of the Eglantyne Jebb who had founded the *Save the Children Fund* in 1919. After graduating in English from Lady Margaret Hall, Oxford, she took the London University Teacher's Diploma in 1913, and became an Assistant English Tutor at Somerville College, Oxford, during the War. In 1919 she became English Lecturer in the Education Department at the University of Birmingham until her appointment to FEI, at an annual salary of £800, from which £70 was deducted for board and lodging. She had not been Froebel trained herself, though her cousin had been so trained, at Stockwell College, more than 30 years earlier. She was a woman of great intelligence, dignity and charm, and, importantly, of vision and determination, and fully in sympathy with the values and ideals of the Froebel movement. She also added a strong academic dimension to the College. She became a close personal friend of Miss Lawrence, and, though some twenty-five years younger, shared similar humane values and convictions. By her own admission, she had been an agnostic since leaving Oxford, and joined the Society of Friends long after retirement, when she was eighty-three.

child, not the class, was the real unit for instruction, and school procedure must be so modified that each child should have liberty to grow in his own way, and to learn by doing'. This represented a substantial advance in national policy towards child-centred education.

However, the thirties were not a propitious time for educational innovation. The great depression was beginning, and Britain had three million unemployed. A courageous leader was needed for FEI, to take its work forward. This new Principal was found in the person of Miss Eglantyne Mary Jebb, MA, who , at 42, was the

Reflecting some twenty years later on her appointment as Principal of FEI, she spoke of her desire to maintain the 'spirit that is part of our Froebelian heritage and has its roots in the respect for human personality which was the centre of Froebel's teaching', and identified three with whom it was associated: Dr Montefiore, Miss Lawrence, and Miss Rosalie Lulham. 'A beautiful, wise tolerance and charity characterised all three of these rare personalities', she said. Eventually, by the end of the decade, three buildings were to be named after them. However, the Froebelian heritage now included a building, Grove House, with serious dry rot. There was massive disruption, including the reconstruction of ceilings, in the front hall and east wing during the summer of 1933 and of the Adam Room and the rest of the House in 1934, as floor joists were replaced by steel girders.

Through the 1920s and early 1930s, the College syllabus entailed examinations at the end of each of the three years, in preparation for the NFU Teacher's Certificate. Most of the 'subject' courses (known as 'ordinary courses') came in the first year:
Year One: English, Mathematics, Nature Knowledge (2 papers), Geography or History;
Year Two: Handwork, Child Hygiene, History of Education, Music *(optional)*;
Year Three: Class Teaching, Principles of Education, Organization & Method, an advanced subject *(optional)*.

During the 1920s, this structure had meant that a student had no experience with children until the third term. A new curriculum was devised during the 1930s, which was finally approved by NFU and by the Board of Education, to allow work with children from the beginning, and to give more time for the 'ordinary courses' by moving year one examinations to year two. These changes, as Miss

A Handwork class, 1930s

Jebb argued, would make a student's training a more coherent whole, rather than an 'academic' year with five examinations separated from studies related to children. Throughout the course, starting in year one, students would observe children at work and play and undertake periods of supervised teaching practice.

Student Reminiscences from the early 1930s

In my day, as one came in the main front door, the room on the left was the library – through that and across a short passage was the main dining hall. We changed into long dresses for Dinner at night. A couple of students each evening had to join the staff at the High Table. They gathered in the front hall and proceeded to enter the dining room together, a slightly scary exercise but good training in manners and small talk to neighbours etc..

My year was accused of not showing proper respect to the third year students. We all used our surnames, only one's closest friends used our first name in the end. My year were told that if we couldn't show more respect for third year students we'd have to call them "Miss".

(R.H. 1930-33)

One had to have permission to go out to a theatre in Central London on a Saturday night from Miss Jebb and to sign out and in when one returned, but one could go down the village any time when one hadn't a lecture.

Once May was over we were allowed to sleep out either on the terrace or in front of the bungalows, with permission from the nurse in charge of sick bay. We had to carry our own camp beds and blankets and clear them by 8 a.m. in the morning when the gardeners came. I also enjoyed sitting about the grass studying, playing tennis or going to Richmond baths.

We were lucky enough to experience both snow and ice during our 3 years. The first for its beauty, the second for skating on the lake, every spare minute.

The Summer term was much nicer as all exams were finished and we could wander round the grounds. We asked boys if we had one near enough, or borrowed day girls' brothers. It was very unlikely for someone to have had a serious boy-friend before they came or during their stay in those days. (H.T. 1930-33)

Our rooms were provided with a bed, desk, chair and chest of drawers – we provided our own linen, curtains, bedspread, mats and easy chair and china and reading lamp, and anything else we liked to take. Each year there was a competition for the most attractive room. We made our own beds and dusted the room. The bathrooms were communal. Third year students moved into Grove House or the surrounding outbuildings. We then had gas fires with a cooking ring and evening cocoa parties were popular. For tea we put out a plate in the dining room with a note of how many were taking tea and we were given milk, bread and butter. Kettles and saucepans we provided ourselves, also jams and cakes etc.. (J.C. 1931-35)

In 1934 also there were a number of significant staffing changes. Miss Mary Saul was appointed as librarian: she was to stay with the College until her retirement 37 years later, having shaped and organised the development of library provision over that time, including the wartime evacuation.

However, a massive blow to the College and former students was the premature and sudden death of Rosalie Lulham, after a short illness on 28th December 1934. Tributes poured in from former students worldwide. She was an extremely well loved and respected tutor, who managed to communicate a sense of wonder and discovery in the natural world to all those whom she taught. She had first joined the staff in 1896, becoming Vice-Principal in 1932. Her book *Introduction to Zoology* (1912) became a standard text in schools and colleges throughout the country. She was dedicated to her work,

Miss Rosalie Lulham

lover of nature), and she started and managed the College's annual Spring Festival, a non-religious celebration of Spring, which was one of the most important events in the College year. She specialised in Field Work, and led scores of expeditions of her students all over the country. She was sorely missed for a long time. More than £1,000 was collected in her memory, which was used to build the Lulham Memorial Rooms, a two-room extension of the first building on the campus put up in 1923, where Rosalie Lulham did much of her teaching. (The whole building is now called Lulham.)

1938 saw the merging of the Froebel Society and the National Froebel Union into the National Froebel Foundation, with the approval of the Board of Education. This combined the energies (and finances) of the two organisations, the one formed for the dissemination of Froebelian principles – becoming less necessary as they became more widely accepted -, and the other formed for maintaining the standards, through syllabus and examination, of the training of Froebel teachers. Mr Montefiore was the benefactor of the Froebel Society and was largely responsible for its survival. The joint organisation, it was hoped, would be more powerful and effective than previously. It certainly became more flexible in its requirements than previously, so that Miss Jebb was able to introduce a 'reformed curriculum' in 1940, with cuts in the number of subjects for examination, more opportunity to specialise, and more time to consider the needs of children.

In the May 1937 issue of *The Link*, Mr Montefiore wrote of Aristotle: 'At the opening of his enquiry into the nature of "happiness" the great Aristotle writes that, however

but maintained a strong sense of social justice as well. She started the Braille Circle in 1909, which over many years supported blind children (and War veterans) by transcribing books into Braille. She recruited students to the Circle who wrote Braille letters to children, collected money and toys, and visited schools for the blind. She started the Natural History Club, which in 1916 became the 'Guild of St Francis' (named after St Francis of Assisi,

The architect's model for the Lawrence Building 1938

much virtue may be a necessary, and even a preponderant, element in happiness, yet "it is clear that happiness requires the addition of external goods, for it is impossible, or at least difficult, for a person to do what is noble unless he is furnished with external means'". With typical judicious discrimination, he argued that Aristotle is both right and wrong, as nobility of spirit does not depend upon wealth. Nevertheless, Miss Jebb was right to argue for a 'fresh instalment of "external goods"'. These were now imminent, in the shape of the Lawrence Building, comprising a library, with residences on three floors above (to replace the shabby bungalows) the Montefiore Wing, comprising teaching rooms with a 'sick wing' and other residences on one floor above (linking Grove House with the Lawrence Building) and modern domestic quarters around the 'kitchen yard'. The cost of the new buildings was £60,000. The College was able to raise only £4,260 by appeals of various sorts. (Eventually the debt was to be written off by the next Chairman, Leonard Montefiore.)

Claude Montefiore laid the Foundation Stone for the Lawrence Building in March 1938. The new buildings were opened by the Lord Mayor of London and the Mayor of Wandsworth on 22 June 1938, shortly after Mr Montefiore's eightieth birthday. He was, however, too ill to attend, and died on 9 July. He had served as Secretary of the Froebel Society from 1884 to 1892, and Chairman from then until his death. He had also been the first Treasurer of FEI, and Chairman from 1917 to 1938, after which, in 1939, his son Leonard took over.

It is hard to overestimate the contribution that Claude Montefiore made to the Froebel Educational Institute. Without his generosity there is no question that an organisation such as FEI, without endowment and built

Leonard Montefiore, c.1940

Claude Montefiore & Miss Jebb, on the way back from Assembly, 1937

own portrait at the front of the dining room – where they hang today – was *not* Mrs Montefiore.) While a student he had been a particular friend of the scholar and classicist, Benjamin Jowett, Master of Balliol, at the end of Jowett's life, and held the ethos and values of Balliol as a model for what a college should aspire to be.

He lived his values. As the *Liberal Jewish Monthly* reported: 'Although he was a wealthy man, he spent little on himself, always travelled third class, patronised the cheapest shops, and would hesitate to ring a bell for fear of troubling the servants. He was very fond of children and used to sprawl on the floor so as not to overawe them with his enormous stature. When walking his dog in his beloved Surrey, he would talk to every passing stranger and to every passing dog'. He visited the FEI College and Schools at least weekly for decades, and gave many talks, formal and informal to students and to children, with whom he was often on the floor, playing. He spoke at College assembly on Friday for many years, usually choosing a reading from an unexpected place. His learning was carried lightly, and was therefore all the more stimulating. His values, like those of Mrs Salis-Schwabe, were not partisan but liberal, ecumenical, progressive, and built on a conviction that freedom and social justice require struggle to achieve and vigilance to protect. And he, like Froebel, saw education as the means to empower that struggle.

on the ideals of committed liberal-minded women, would never have been able to start, let alone survive. As FEI was a purely private venture, no grants were available for tuition until 1918, and no capital grants for building were possible until 1945. He donated an asset which is worth many millions of pounds today. But he gave much more than finance (and a library) to the College and Schools. He brought a cultured and discriminating intellect, leavened by a rich sense of humour. (He used to joke with students that the glamorous portrait of Julia Schwabe which partnered his

Student Reminiscences from the later 1930s

The beautiful grounds, magnificent old cedar tree, the lake, the grotto, (on which we often had picnics) and the lime walk. We walked down the lime walk and crossed the field to use the Roehampton Club swimming pool. In return the club members used our pool for skating, when it froze. I remember going down the lime walk one evening, to peer into the grounds of the Sacred Heart, to watch the badgers – a magical experience. (L.E.F. 1934-37)

Most of us had bicycles; there was no College vehicle for transporting us to schools for Teaching Practice. It was only 2d from Grove House to Hammersmith on the bus. If your school was too far away to get back to College for lunch you were given 1s 6d (71/2p) – at the local Lyons you could make a profit! We liked teaching at a big Fulham elementary school (Munster Road) where the Headmaster gave us malt, and warned us when our supervisor was coming to watch us teach. At the end of dinner each evening the Senior Student read out requests for the loan of pictures or equipment, such as 40 pairs of compasses, for other students to take to their lessons next day. (Sr. B.G. & C.C. 1935-38)

Then at college we also walked down the lime walk in the summer, and I can still remember the smell of the blossoms. And then we either got through the fence or over it – or maybe there was a gate, I don't remember – and we went next door to the Roehampton Polo Club to watch the polo games. One day we found a notice on the notice board saying that students must wear hats when watching polo games. So in the next college skit, there were students dressed in swimsuits but correctly dressed for polo, wearing hats and, I believe, gloves.
(C.R. 1935-38)

1939-1945: Evacuation – Knebworth House and Offley Place

THE College had enjoyed the new facilities and Library for only one year when, in 1939, in common with other schools and colleges in London, it was under government orders to evacuate. Grove House had been let for the duration to the National Provincial Bank for a rent of £350 p.a., and Templeton had been let for the same annual sum to the Bank of England, though the bank sublet the house in 1942 to the Norwegian Government, when it became a hospital for Norwegian servicemen and sailors. The Courts were let to a firm of London accountants, and in 1940, Colet Gardens School, the original home of FEI, was let to Pickfords as a furniture depository. (The school wing was severely damaged by a bomb in September 1940).

The hot afternoon of Saturday 9th September 1939 saw the Grove House School bus (or 'tumbril', as it was being called by some of its occupants) set off, with a small group of College staff, heading for Knebworth House in Hertfordshire, the ancestral home (since 1490) of Victor, 2nd Earl of Lytton, who had placed his home at the disposal of the College rent free for the duration of the

war. Numerous furniture vans carrying beds, tables, books, and other equipment had preceded it. The National Provincial Bank had already moved into Grove House.

Lord Lytton had been Governor of Bengal 1922-27, and was the grandson of Edward Bulwer-Lytton, the Victorian MP and novelist, perhaps now most famous for *The Last Days of Pompeii* (1834). His father, as Viceroy of India, had proclaimed Queen Victoria Empress of India in 1877. His wife was Pamela Plowden, a close friend of Winston Churchill (who had often visited Knebworth house in the 1930s and made a painting of the Banqueting Hall). The couple continued to live at the Manor House nearby during the war, and often met with FEI students.

First year students were located at Offley Place, the home of Colonel Arthur Acland, a Queen Anne house standing on a hill in 30 acres, located ten miles from Knebworth, and supervised there by Miss Hutchinson, English tutor and formerly Warden of Templeton. Second and third years were billeted mainly in the grand surroundings of Knebworth itself, with its imposing

Knebworth House, 1939

Offley Place, 1939

Knebworth Banqueting Hall, with College dining room furniture

Knebworth Picture Gallery, used as the students' Common Room

from Knebworth. Within a year it had 46 boarders and 37 day pupils, and was calling itself 'The Froebel Preparatory School at Little Gaddesden'. The Grove House School closed down, as the children were all under eleven, and there were too few whose parents wished them to evacuate with the school. Miss Bow, the headmistress, rejoined the College staff at Knebworth. The free kindergartens which Miss Lawrence set up in Notting Hill and St Pancras had evacuated to Tunbridge Wells in Kent and Eydon in Nottinghamshire (only 20 miles from Knebworth) respectively.

Wartime life for students was, however, much grimmer than the above description of Knebworth House might imply. The overwhelming memory of students was of cold, as it was impossible to heat such grand rooms given wartime fuel restrictions. Even baths had to be shared, sometimes four or five using the same water (sometimes in sequence, sometimes together, we understand), and no more often than twice a week. Although there was a four-poster bed which it is claimed Queen Elizabeth I had slept in, most students were obliged to sleep on uncomfortable and collapsible camp beds. Food was, of course, rationed. But somehow, many students and staff testify, it brought the college closer together through shared struggle. All students had bicycles, which were a necessity for getting to a new set of schools for teaching practice. There was a station at Knebworth, though some distance from the House, which offered cheap travel to London if you travelled before 6.00 a.m. on a 'workman's ticket'.

Academic facilities at Offley Place and Knebworth House were largely improvised. Adequate library books were brought up from the new Lawrence Library, but

rooms, gothic fantasy architecture, suits of armour, four-poster beds, Lutyens-designed gardens, and 250 acres of parkland, or at the nearby Lytton Lodge, a short walk away. A few staff and students stayed in billets in Knebworth village. The Colet Gardens Demonstration School, with 28 children and Miss Barbara Priestman as headmistress, eventually in January 1940 settled in Little Gaddesden, also in Hertfordshire, about fifteen miles

facilities for Art and Handwork were very limited. However, botany, zoology and geography seem to have gained by the relocation in the countryside, thanks to the genuine Froebelian enthusiasm for the natural world exhibited by staff and students alike. The 'reformed curriculum' introduced in 1940, which had allowed more course-work assessment, was an appropriate innovation in the current circumstances.

During the heavy bombing on London in the summer of 1940 (the Battle of Britain), a high explosive shell fell at Grove House near the Art Room, shattering the windows and doors, an oil bomb fell in front of Grove House School, shattering the windows and covering the school with dirty oil (which did not ignite), the historic garden wall in front of Templeton was smashed to pieces, and Colet Gardens school building suffered a direct hit from an incendiary bomb which burnt out the roof. The playing fields at Grove House were pitted with bomb holes but were anyway planted with vegetables for the war effort and were being tended by Mr Longhurst the College gardener (known to students and staff as 'Longhurst', who lived in the Lodge by the Roehampton Lane entrance. Lytton Lodge actually received three high explosive near-misses, which brought down ceilings and shattered windows and doors, but no-one was hurt and repairs were soon completed.

1942 was the 50th anniversary of the founding of FEI, but there were no celebrations, given the privations of war and the unknown future. 1942 was a bleak period in the war. After the attack on Pearl Harbour the previous December, Japan was advancing across most of the Far East and South Pacific and was threatening Australia;

Stalingrad was still under siege from the Germans, and it was not until October 1942 that the Eighth Army victory under Montgomery at El Alamein gave some hope that the tide might have turned. Teachers were leaving the profession in large numbers to take up other forms of war service which seemed more directly related to the war and were perhaps more exciting. The Board of Education published a circular which stated:

No woman teacher should feel any doubt where her duty lies; unless she has some special qualification which is of particular value to some other vital branch of the national war effort, she will be undertaking the best form of service in her power by continuing her teaching work.

Miss Jebb reminded present and former students of the duty 'which, as Froebelians, and as those who have had the privilege of a full training, we owe to the children during these difficult war years'.

Dalcroze Eurhythmics at Knebworth

Student Reminiscences of Evacuation

I suppose one's chief memory of Lytton Lodge was serving our own meals and washing up afterwards. In London we had had waitresses, and numerous kitchen staff.

One hot sunny weekend we watched many lorries pass along the road – we learnt later that they were convoys carrying our troops back from Dunkirk.

On our journeys from Lytton Lodge across the Park for lectures at Knebworth House we had to pass an anti-aircraft unit – a friendly crowd – and the only men we ever saw!!
(O.P. 1937-40)

At Knebworth were 2nd and 3rd year students only. We slept 5 or 6 to a bedroom and took it in turns to sleep in the Four Poster. The other beds were canvas camp ones. It was very cold in the winter but we were allowed fuel for a fire one day a month. We could augment this by gathering wood.

There were 16 to our bathroom and at first we queued up outside but we soon decided that we all looked alike and in we went. We were allowed two 6 inch baths a week but by joining up with someone from another 2 nights and getting in together (there was plenty of room) we got extra.

At Knebworth we took it in turns to fire-watch in pairs. Students did the first watch at night then had to wake a member of staff, who later had to wake another couple of students for the early morning stint. Miss Jebb gave us the use of her study and we were provided with an oil stove, saucepan, milk and cocoa and biscuits.

During the winter the lake used to freeze over and a number of us used to enjoy skating. Lord Lytton was often there too and would enquire after our families and help anyone who was trying to learn to skate. *(P.C. 1938-41)*

The only real crime was waste. I remember all hell let loose when someone put a slice of bread and marg in the bin. We shared books, baths and bedclothes. I remember the patter of mice running round the rooms at night: one ate a sweet through my dressing gown pocket, leaving a large hole. *(D.G. 1938-41)*

This was a time of learning to be flexible and resourceful. We all had bikes, so 'Auntie Bell', one of the craft tutors, organised the making of bike-stands. Much discussion, teacher learning alongside the students. The stands, when at last put together, were a triumph, lasting the duration of the war, possibly far beyond. Final exams – then it was all over. Not so the Froebel Experience. After three years which took in both Grove House and Knebworth we were turned into the world as qualified teachers. But I believe it went much further than that. What we were given by those enlightened and dedicated women was a whole philosophy of life. It has always been there for me during a long, active life. *(M.H. 1938-41)*

Lessons and lectures were delivered all over the ground floor of the house. There was the Oak Room, a lovely oak-panelled room in the far corner of the house where we had Hygiene lessons from a Dr. Cadman, a very interesting woman with many stories to tell from her medical days who always kept our attention. She had specialised in Radiology but her hands had been burnt and she could no longer practise medicine. There was the Great Hall which could take a large number of students for a lecture but had to be cleared quickly for we ate in there too.

The Picture Gallery was a long room which opened out into a square at the end. We had assemblies in there and used it as a sort of common room. There was a fire which was lit in the evenings but not many of us could get round it. There was the Minstrels Gallery over the end of the Great Hall, many tutorials took place up there.

Teaching Practices were difficult for the staff to arrange and it was amazing what they managed to get for us.

There was another 'Home' where we spent some time. This was for under fives and was situated in a large country house. The owner still lived in part of it. It was full of little children who had been bombed out of London and most of them had lost their parents. They were pathetic and bewildered; they displayed many behaviour problems which were not understood by the nurses who cared for them. One little boy used to hide under a sofa and pinch the ankles of anyone who sat on it. I think he was the child who, when the owner of the house came to say good night to the children refused to do so and was shut up in a dark cupboard to consider his sins. This was a child who had suffered the bombing and had lost both his parents. It was really a dreadful place. When we arrived on our first visit we were welcomed into what had been the rather lovely drawing room, now stripped of its furniture and thirty children sitting on chamber pots. They had to sit there until they performed and were severely punished if they wet or soiled themselves. We students complained to the college staff about the horrors and I think something was done. There was an appalling epidemic of impetigo, those poor children had sores in their heads and even in their mouths and until we complained were not treated. We had to stop visiting because of the infection. The one subject that we did not study at all was Religious Education. Many of us felt that this was a great lack. It was the one subject that we were obliged to teach in Primary School and we were totally unprepared for it. (S.M. 1938-41)

An excellent scheme designed to include Resident and Day students and students from the two years ahead of us was the Major, Minor, Minimus plan. The "Majors" were 3rd year students, the "Minors" 2nd year students and the "Minimi" 1st years. This plan cut across the years and offered great scope for

helpful advice and counselling. When we first arrived at FEI as 1st year students we were introduced to our personal Major and Minor. At tea gatherings we met other Major, Minor and Minimus trios and soon we got to know students right across the three years. The impact of those years made a profound impression, demanded an assessment of priorities and equipped us with the ability to face the after-war years when Froebel trained teachers invaded the state system. (M.R. 1938-41)

A typical day began with breakfast at 8 a.m., and then lectures from 9.30 to 12.30. Lunch was at 1 p.m. and the afternoon was free. We had lectures again from 4.30 to 6.30 and dinner was at 7 p.m.. There were ten or a dozen staff living at Knebworth, approachable and helpful and only slightly eccentric! The Principal, Miss Jebb, was very highly regarded.

As there was a danger of incendiary bombs being dropped, we had a rota of 'firewatchers'. Two students sat up from 10 p.m. till midnight, one member of staff from midnight till 5 a.m. and two more students from 5 a.m. till 7 a.m.. (I.A. 1939-42)

At Knebworth House we ate in the banqueting hall (our individual butter rations etc. labelled to claim from side tables). We had P.T. and Speech Training on the Fives Court, Art and Handwork in the village hall, and private study in the very lovely library. Lord Lytton visited and talked to us, urging us not to block up the plumbing by too much hair-washing, and he skated with us on the frozen lake.

As Senior Student in my final year I was allotted Lord Lytton's room to share with two friends. We had a beautiful view over the maze and formal gardens, a huge bath in the bedroom, and a hatch which opened into Lady Lytton's bathroom which adjoined her bedroom, now shared by five. We did energetic early morning exercises to the radio.

One evening three of us walked back from the station after a day out to find everyone sitting in the long back corridors – there had been an air raid warning whilst we were on the train and we knew nothing of it. (E.M. 1939-42)

In the early days at Offley, I remember Miss Hutchinson reading us Howard's End in the dark evenings as we sat round on the floor in the beautiful common room. I am sure she enjoyed it but we did too! She was our Head of House. (M.H.S. 1939-42)

I well remember playing the 'cello (badly) in the Minstrel Gallery for 'Comus' in which Lord Lytton took part, and was the FEI's Farewell Event to Knebworth House.
When my boyfriend, an Army Officer, now my husband, called at Knebworth House to see me immediately prior to D-Day, Miss Jebb insisted on interviewing John before we could meet! Since then, in appropriate circles, John has proudly announced "I knew Miss Jebb"! (S.M. 1942-45)

We were always hungry and went into Hitchin when we could to buy a sausage or tomato on toast at the Copper Kettle. It cost one shilling and ninepence old money – at the time!
We used to get up very early on Saturdays and take a workman's train ticket to London where after breakfast at the Quality Inn or a Lyons Corner House we put our stools down for 1/- to queue for the gallery at the theatre, forerunner of the National Theatre.
Here we saw for one or two shillings all the great actors of the day, Laurence Olivier, Vivien Leigh, Peggy Ashcroft, etc.. This was an education for life. It would not be fair to say that these Saturdays, including rehearsals for concerts at the Albert Hall for one shilling to see Sir Henry Wood, Sir Thomas Beecham, Sir Adrian Boult conducting, were my favourite memories of life at the Froebel Institute – all in all it was a great experience. (V.K. 1943-46)

INTERNAL EXAMINATION

NATIONAL FROEBEL FOUNDATION

This is to Certify
that *Elizabeth Margaret Denne-Cox*
having been trained at
THE FROEBEL EDUCATIONAL INSTITUTE
an institution approved by the National Froebel Foundation, has been duly awarded a

TEACHER'S CERTIFICATE (A)
of the First Class

STATEMENT SHOWING THE DEGREE OF PROFICIENCY IN THE DIFFERENT SUBJECTS

Compulsory Subjects

ENGLISH LITERATURE *Exempt* CLASS			PRINCIPLES OF		
NATURE KNOWLEDGE			EDUCATION	II	CLASS
SECTION I	II	CLASS	ORGANISATION &		
SECTION II	I	CLASS	METHOD	I	CLASS
ELEMENTS OF			HYGIENE	I	CLASS
MATHEMATICS	II	CLASS	HISTORY OF		
GEOGRAPHY		CLASS	EDUCATIONAL IDEAS	I	CLASS
OR			HANDWORK	II	CLASS
HISTORY	I	CLASS	CLASS TEACHING	II	CLASS

Optional Subjects

ORDINARY			ADVANCED		
MUSIC	I	CLASS	LITERATURE	I	CLASS
ART		CLASS	GEOGRAPHY		CLASS
RELIGIOUS KNOWLEDGE		CLASS	HISTORY		CLASS

R. Halley
CHAIRMAN

Date *September, 1942*

monkhouse
SECRETARY

An NFF Certificate, 1942

By September 1942, one whole cohort of students had finished their three years' training 'in exile', and in that month Miss Jebb took some of them, together with a group of staff, back for an afternoon's visit to Grove House. Feelings were confused, for, in Miss Jebb's words,

The changes have certainly not been all loss. It is not only that for many of us this Hertfordshire countryside…and the charm of our immediate surroundings both at Offley and at Knebworth have laid fast hold of our affections, but in the day to day routine of our College life, sharing as we do now more intimately in the domestic duties of house, kitchen and pantry, we seem to get to know each other better and to have a closer sense of fellowship. The quickening interest also in social and educational affairs which is abroad in the whole country has had its marked repercussions on College life…

In 1942 the College was required to introduce a shortened two-year course for older students, and reduce the entry age for the three-year course to 17 years. By 1943 nobody over 18 on 1st October was allowed to register for the three-year course, and nobody over 19 on that date could even enter for the two-year course. The 'call-up' was swallowing up the available human resources. Although applications to the College held up well, the student body was deprived of its leavening of mature students who made a special contribution to College life. It was hoped that after the war students who had completed the two-year course would return for a year to complete the full NFF Certificate

Hill House today

In the summer of 1943, Colonel Acland offered Offley Place for sale, and FEI decided to purchase it, partly to avoid the disruption of moving out during wartime. It was to remain with FEI until 1953, when the Hertfordshire LEA took it over. It remained a training college, specialising in Rural Studies, until 1961, when it was closed by ministerial decision and became a residential LEA Teachers' Centre. Miss Lawrence, now 81 years of age, donated a large quantity of furniture and books in order to furnish the house after the Acland furniture was removed. She also offered her country home, Hill House, Kelvedon, in Essex, in trust to FEI for educational use after the war. (It was in 1943 occupied by the army, and after the war FEI passed the lease to the Save the Children Fund, who used it as a country recuperation home for small groups of disadvantaged children aged 7-11, not only from war-torn Europe, but also from British city slums.). 'One wonders', mused Miss Jebb, 'if any other school or college, in the fifth year of this devastating and destructive war, can place on record such a tale of gifts which enrich the present and open up fresh vistas for the future'. Morale was rising.

The exciting topic of educational debate during 1943 was, however, the Education Bill which was to become the 1944 Act (the 'Butler' Act) in the following year. It was judged to rest on a truly Froebelian conception of education, in that it rejected 'efficient elementary instruction in the 3Rs' as any longer an acceptable definition of primary education. Class sizes of 50 were deplored, as conducive to 'mass production' rather than education. The main provisions of the Act when passed were:

• the Board of Education was replaced by a Minister who was to control LEAs (which were reduced in number from 315 to 146);
• there would be secondary education for all;
• no fees could be charged in any publicly-maintained school;
• state education provision would be in 'three progressive stages, to be known as primary education, secondary education, and further education';
• each LEA was obliged to submit a development plan for primary, secondary and further education;
• there would be a daily collective act of worship in all state primary and secondary schools, with a conscience clause allowing withdrawal;

• secondary provision would be in accordance with 'age, ability, and aptitude', and there would be three types of secondary school – grammar, modern, and technical (these could, exceptionally, be under one roof);
• there would be a selection test at age 11.

This was a radical set of reforms indeed. The task of training colleges now would be to recruit trainees in order that vacancies might be filled with trained people, and that class sizes might be reduced. The success of D-Day in June 1944 raised morale even further. The end of the war was nearing and the task of social reconstruction beginning.

In July 1944, a few weeks after the D-Day landings, and as flying bombs were dropping on London, Miss Lawrence died, aged 82, after a short illness. This was exactly fifty years after she had joined the staff, on the foundation of FEI in Colet Gardens. She had guided or influenced FEI through most of that period, which began at a time when there was no education beyond the age of eleven for 98% of children in Britain, and ended with the 1944 Education Act which made school compulsory for all up to age 14. The period contained two world wars, a financial slump, and the Great Depression. Miss Lawrence combined determination with personal modesty, and towards the end of her life would repeatedly say of Mr Montefiore, 'It was all owing to him', though she herself embodied the inspiration and the authority which was the driving force behind the early years of FEI. One member of the FEI Governing Body wrote in 1945:

She was indeed the rock on which the College was built, but her intuition leapt forward. As she said, she lived "always five years ahead". Her wonderful business instinct went hand-in-hand with vision and complete unworldliness. She was serenely oblivious of regulations and red tape, but she respected form and tradition, only however, as a background for the spontaneous expression of individuality.

Miss Lawrence

It had been Miss Lawrence's conviction (and Mr Montefiore's money) that led the College to become residential, and she had established the 'Students' House Committee', which became the nucleus of the Students' Union. She had a strong sense of social justice (the 'nearly-free' Challoner Street school was due to her efforts, as were the two free kindergartens which FEI set up in Notting Hill and St Pancras), and an empathy with the thinking of young children. She understood instinctively what was valuable in people and in things. She recounted in a letter in 1943 the following story about her childhood in New York:

> *When I was a child in New York an uncle took some of us children to an enormous and grand toy shop, and told us we could have any toys we wanted. We were surrounded by all sorts of grand things. I remember the thing I wanted most of all was a little sailor boy with a broken arm, from which sawdust was escaping. It appealed to me deep down and I would have nothing else. Going home I held the sailor up to the stagecoach window, so that he could see what was going on outside. I am sure that my sailor could not have cost more than a few pence, but he was rich in history and joy for me.*

Miss Jebb wrote in the National Froebel Foundation *Bulletin* in September 1944, that though 'new developments in psychology and in our social outlook have altered our educational perspective and methods,…Miss Lawrence's influence on education, like all spiritual influences, is beyond the compass of our measuring sticks'.

TEN

1945-1950: Postwar Return to Grove House

AS the war in Europe drew to a close, plans were made to return to war-damaged Grove House. Yet more dry rot was found, and this made using Grove House difficult for nearly a year. Temporary signs were everywhere, as there were so many new staff and students unfamiliar with the premises. Recruitment was very high in September 1945, since the Ministry of Education was urging all training colleges to take extra students, yet the buildings were in no state to accommodate them. Repairs needed Government permits, and it was a year before most of the repair work could be completed with the materials available. More staff were also appointed. Whereas numbers in training in 1944 at Knebworth and Offley had been 161, in September 1945 the total was 284. Of these, 199 were resident at Grove House, 35 were day students, and 50 were at Offley.

Knebworth was relinquished in 1945, but Offley Place, which FEI had bought in 1943 when Colonel Acland declared his intention to sell, was retained as a 'Training Centre'. From September 1945, it was planned that students would spend their first two years at Offley and then move to Roehampton for their final year. However, the need for teachers was so desperate that the Ministry persuaded FEI to provide a two-year training course at Offley from 1947, with a new intake of 50 students every second year. This worked until 1953, when the cost of running two campuses became too much for FEI and Offley was sold to the Hertfordshire Local Education Authority. The Authority invested in new buildings and administered the College until 1961, when it became a Teachers' Centre.

Back at Roehampton, the Demonstration School reopened in adjacent premises at Ibstock Place in October 1946, which had been purchased for £40,000. Meanwhile, in June, the former premises in Colet Gardens had been sold to Sadlers Wells Ballet as a training school for £12,000, and the headquarters of FEI moved to Templeton. During 1946-47, the scars of war damage were gradually eliminated from Grove House and the estate. Bomb shelters remained, but bomb damage to the playing fields and tennis courts was repaired, and the Row was re-occupied. Visitors to the college during the year included Sir David Maxwell-Fife, who spoke on the Nuremberg Trials, and two concerts were given in the Adam Room by Solomon, the concert pianist. Life seemed to be returning to normal.

Miss Jebb in her study

The 1944 Education Act (the 'Butler' Act), had restructured the education system by abolishing School Boards, by defining three stages of state educational provision (primary, secondary and further), and by introducing selection at 11 plus. These far-reaching changes affected Froebel-trained teachers directly. Many lost their jobs as newly-defined secondary schools closed their primary departments and elementary schools changed their status, and they were forced to seek new jobs in the new primary schools. More importantly, the primary schools began preparing their pupils to pass the all-important 11 plus exam. Passing meant, for 20% of the age-cohort, going on to the (new) grammar schools and taking further qualifications at 16 and/or 18; failure meant going on to the secondary modern school, taking no further qualifications. Examinations and testing were coming to be important issues in public sector education now. A Report on Ibstock Place for 1949-50 includes the following acknowledgement of the eleven plus:

Now we are just setting out on the Spring Term of 1950, intent on taking the County Common Entrance Examination at eleven plus, even though many of our children will not be able to make use of it. We feel that they should take it in case, in the future, they ever should be so placed that they would want a County School education. It means that the next spring term is rather too full with examinations, as the London County Council examination is held in January, and the Girls' Common Entrance for Independent Schools in February, but the boys' Public School Entrance is not until June.

Nationally in 1945 there were 83 recognised training colleges, with approximately 10,000 students, and 22

university training departments, with about 5,000 students. Of the 83 colleges, 54 were voluntary (27 Anglican, 16 non-denominational, 9 Roman Catholic, and 2 Methodist) and 29 were maintained by Local Education Authorities. The majority had fewer than 150 students. Most colleges offered only two-year training courses, though eleven domestic science colleges and six physical education colleges offered three-year courses. In addition the Froebel colleges, of which there were now five, offered three-year courses, leading to the NFF Teacher's Certificate for internal students. They were:

• Froebel Educational Institute, SW15
• The Clapham and Streatham Hill Training College, SW2
• Maria Grey Training College, NW6
• Rachel McMillan Training College, SE8
• The Training College, Bedford.

At FEI the first year for all students was self-funded, and the ability to support this continued to be an implicit entry criterion. There were no examinations in Year One, but students' work was open to inspection by NFF, and the College kept informal records of progress. Students were grouped according to whether they were training for Nursery and Infant School (ages 2-7) or Junior School (ages 5-11+). (This latter range was separated shortly afterwards into age ranges 5-8½ and 7-11½.)

All subjects were started in Year One, but they were not examined until years Two or Three. Basic school curriculum subjects were spread throughout the three years. Professional subjects included: Hygiene, Practice of Teaching (examined by the Ministry of Education as well as by NFF), Principles and Practice of Education, and Physical Training (examined by the Ministry of Education). Special subjects, of which students were allowed to take three 'of which one only may be Advanced', comprised: Art and Handwork, Music, Nature Study, English Literature, Geography, History, Mathematics (Primary students only), Religious Knowledge, and Social Studies (Infant students only). For the first time in 1947, students would spend a whole term in their third year on teaching practice, using the college 'as their base and their arsenal', as Miss Jebb expressed it.

This was basically the pattern of the curriculum until the momentous event in 1949, when, as a result of the implementation of the McNair Report (1944), Froebel Institute College became part of the newly established Area Training Organisation centred on the new University of London Institute of Education, which, starting with thirty, eventually was to comprise thirty-six colleges in and around London. McNair himself had argued against full integration of training colleges within university departments of education. He wrote:

It must not be forgotten that for the vast majority of the quarter of a million or more of the teachers needed by our schools, the predominant qualities required, in addition to a good general education, are an interest in, and an understanding of, children, and a desire to live one's life with them and help them to develop themselves on the right lines – qualities which have no connection with university standards at all, and are apt not to receive due recognition and encouragement in an academic atmosphere, but will be adequately safeguarded in the training colleges.

He preferred regional academic associations, and proposed the establishment of a 'common professional qualification' for qualified teacher status, 'in the interest of unifying the teaching profession', to be controlled by enhanced Joint Boards. This was to mean co-ordination of syllabuses, though they might differ in the detail of content, and common examinations and assessment of students among colleges. McNair also recommended a three-year training programme for 18-year olds entering training colleges (although this was not implemented until 1960). These two factors – loss of control of examination and assessment (and effectively thereby of the heart of the syllabus) and extension of the training period nationally to three years – were, slowly but inexorably, to prove lethal to the distinctive identity of Froebel Institute College.

It was still the case in the immediate post-war years that

Olive Garnett with students at Clandon, 1965

College staff regularly taught pupils at the Demonstration School, Ibstock Place. This relationship was built into the very structure of FEI, but would not survive beyond 1960. The following reminiscence by one long-standing member of College staff, Olive Garnett, who taught at FEI for nearly 40 years, from 1926 to 1965, gives some flavour of surviving pedagogic practice at the time. She recalled taking an Ibstock class of 7-8 year-olds 'one sunny but windy afternoon' in the late 1940s for a walk to find out where the water flowing in a ditch went to:

Eventually we discovered that it tumbled into Beverley Brook, of which it was a tributary. On our way we had stayed to watch ploughs at work, for war-time farming still continued in Richmond Park. The ploughs were followed by flocks of gulls. On our way back to school we paused at the Park gates to look back. Someone said, 'The gulls are still flying'. Another, 'The ploughs are still working'. Another, 'And the wind is still blowing'. Then a boy who could not read remarked, 'It's rather like a poem, isn't it'. It seems to illustrate how things that might be separated under subjects are inseparable parts of a natural whole when children are absorbed in a reality. Much that was geographical followed from this, including work with maps. For instance, it was discovered that Beverley Brook is itself a tributary of the Thames; and this led to a demand for a map which showed 'the whole of the Thames and all its tributaries, and all the tributaries of the tributaries.

This is truly child-centred education – *but* the boy aged 7-8 could not read. This would be the issue – basic skills – that would eventually cause demand for change in pedagogic training and practice.

The College received a visitation from the Institute of Education in December 1948 (and Offley in May 1949), as a result of which recognition of FEI was approved for four years in the first instance. Nevertheless, the Report noted that the Governing Body had no representation from staff, and that the Principal was not a member, and recommended that 'new blood' be sought from time to time. It criticised the arrangements for teaching practice, which allowed students only two weeks during the whole of their first year at the end of the summer term. It criticised the syllabus for too much concentration on subject study and not enough on 'the needs and interests of children and the methods by which they learn'. One member of the visiting panel expressed the view that the association with the NFF was 'due to historical and sentimental causes', and only the University should control the examination. The Report sat on the fence with regard to the claimed special value of the longer, more thorough and less hurried three-year NFF programme. It did however, contain the bombshell sentence: 'In the case of this College, its educational outlook does not appear to be any more specifically Froebelian than that of any other Training College which prepares students for work with young children', but followed it up with an appeasing 'This, of course, may be because the training in these other Colleges is largely in the hands of people who themselves have taken the Froebel training'.

In the summer of 1949 FEI hosted a three-week international conference, jointly sponsored by the Ministry of Education and supported by the Foreign Office, entitled: 'The study and discussion of recent developments in the education of children between two and twelve years with special reference to present-day movements in Primary education in England'. Not a catchy title, but delegates came from more than a dozen countries, including the Minister of Education, George Tomlinson, who gave an address and had tea on the lawn with the Principal and delegates. The topic was of growing importance, and would eventually, eighteen years later, be the subject of a full Government Report, 'Children and their Primary Schools' (the 'Plowden Report').

As a result of this conference, Miss Jebb introduced into the curriculum 'Exploratory Work' for first year students, with emphasis on 'the observation and teaching of children' and 'independent reading and investigation', so that they might experience learning by enquiry and discovery ('the natural way of learning'), without regard to subject divisions. This was to remain on the syllabus through to the 1970s.

Student Reminiscences from the later 1940s

I had a room in a little sort of outplace called New Court. It was a very small room, but it had a gas fire and a little gas ring which made me feel very comfortable, and a wash basin. Fortunately that part of the college was heated by gas and it was very difficult, in fact it was impossible, to turn gas off during the war; apparently if you turn it off, the pipes get air in them and you get explosions. The college got bigger. I'm not quite sure how it did it, but it was bigger and there seemed to be a great many more staff, and after we'd been there a few weeks, or possibly one term, they managed to get more domestic staff in, and some time during that second year all the washing-up and laying of tables stopped and there were special people to do that.
The last year of my time there was the year of the Great Freeze, in 1947.
When I was on the teaching practice there was a very nice school called the Lady Eleanor Hollis, a very nice and friendly staff, and the class I was supposed to be with was in the hall. It was quite a large hall and it had got, I think, one oil lamp in it which didn't make much difference. I had been taught that you shouldn't teach children with your coat on because that makes the children feel insecure. So being immensely conscientious I refused to put my coat on, whereas everybody else never took their coats off. So I got a great deal colder than was really necessary. The children there were very nice and the work was really very easy and the staff were very helpful. (A.F. 1944-47)

The teaching at FEI I remember as being superb. So much enthusiasm, as when Miss Garnett took us out on the hills with a large blackboard to learn and teach the fundamentals of map-reading, and digging in dark pits looking for whale teeth etc..
(W.V. 1945-47)

The majority of the students were fairly young, around 18 years of age and from sheltered backgrounds, probably straight from boarding school. But things were changing with more mature students released from wartime jobs and the armed forces and finding the opportunity to train. Roehampton seemed to me to be a good cross-section of students from the Honourables to the miners' daughters with a sprinkling of foreigners. (A.S. 1945-48)

We had various foreign students. I remember some from India, Egypt, America, Singapore, Nigeria, France, (Nadine Guiton who sadly died during our first Summer vacation), Belgium, Barbados, Germany, the Channel Isles, Isle of Man, Scilly Isles, if I remember rightly.
(N.A. 1946-49)

Our second term at College was one that none of us would forget, for we experienced all the hardships of the 1947 winter – with snow, ice and freezing temperatures from early January until early March. On top of the weather problems, the Labour Government was facing transport strikes – so there were delays in delivering food to shops, and fuel – which was in short supply – was not being distributed to power stations. There were power cuts throughout the country and there was no heat or light between 9 a.m. and noon, and 2 p.m. and 4 p.m. each day. One entry in my diary records that Templeton only had enough cake left for one day. Hot water was also "rationed" and no-one could have baths for about a week, until more coke was delivered. According to my diary, the worst day was 20th February – "the sky all day remained a varying shade of orange (the result of "smog" which was common at that time). It was so dark it was like a prolonged twilight. Electricity cuts made work almost impossible, and at 10 a.m. we could only see to read in the Common Room by the light of the open fire. In the Library people worked by candlelight and at Templeton we used to retire

and we huddled up with rugs and blankets with hot water bottles. The food was very scanty all day".
The roads were so icy that it was about five weeks before we could use our cycles to get around – and day to day living was quite a struggle. Our basic rations, which we collected each week from the kitchen, were 2 oz. of butter, 2 oz. of margarine and 2 oz. of sugar, plus a small pot of jam for the month. We were allowed two slices of bread and a small jug of milk each day for tea, and the bonus was a small bag of NAMCO each week (dried milk and cocoa which we mixed with boiling water to make a welcome hot drink). (M.D. 1946-49)

It's not easy now to realise how short of everything we were. Every bit of paper was written on – no margins. Drawings were made on small sheets of paper. Children could be painting on whitewashed newspaper. All art materials were handed out grudgingly. Pencils and pens in schools were counted back in after use. No biros – but pen and ink!
For many of us, if not all, the "ordinary" schools were a shock. Often grim Victorian buildings, no painting or upkeep during the war, sometimes a bomb crater still in the playground, outside toilets, crammed classrooms and lack of books, paper, etc.. Every school had an unmistakable smell of chalk, disinfectant and children. Some children I remember clearly, for example Yvonne, undersized, youngest of a grown-up family who went home for dinner – 'bread and scrape' – so she could wash up, make beds, etc. for those out at work. Then Pat, very bright, sister at grammar school – both locked out most evenings till parents returned from the pub. School, I suppose, was a warm haven where she could sleep on her desk. What happened to them all? Speech training was an afternoon lecture, in which I was, rightly, often in trouble for being late. Maybe I was subconsciously putting off the moments spent standing in a circle saying "Coo, ooo, what shall I do? I only have one egg, I ought to have two" –

enunciating clearly and exaggeratedly – and no laughing! (E.J.L. 1946-49)

Miss Jebb used to interview each of us privately at the end of term and read us the comments and criticisms of our lecturers. She would stand on the hearthrug with her back to the blazing open fire in her study, surreptitiously raising her skirt a little so that she could feel the warmth on her legs. "Ah, um, er Miss Hassell", she said at the end of my first term. "I don't think we have been working quite as hard as we ought, have we?" (K.H. 1946-49)

Academic matters were important and I liked the fact that we were developing our education as well as the practical side of teaching in the classroom. We had to give work in on time, but I don't think the staff were severe if a little late. You always felt you could ask for help if you were in need. (M.B. 1948-51)

Dinner was a formal affair. The staff, presided over by Miss Jebb, would enter the dining hall when the college had assembled. (3rd years sitting at tables nearest the High Table and 1st years farthest away.) Grace (in Latin) would be said by Miss Jebb, all would be seated and dinner served. When the meal was finished a final Grace would be said and the college would stand as the staff left the room. Dress, although not formal evening wear, was expected to be neat and appropriate.
Coupon Nights. Students were allowed one 'coupon night' a term. This was permission to spend the night away from college. Permission had to be obtained from Miss Jebb, who would expect to be told why the coupon night was needed.
Men (including brothers and fathers). Men were only allowed in students' rooms on Saturday and Sunday afternoons. As I remember it this rule was, on the whole, well observed, but I do remember stories about young men hiding in wash rooms and under beds from time to time.

The Summer Ball. This was a formal affair – black ties and long evening dresses. We had to submit a list of our partners' names before the event, and on the night each young man had to be introduced to Miss Jebb.
Wirelesses. Wirelesses were only permitted in the second and third years. This, we were told, was to keep noise levels down. There was, I think, a wireless in the common room.
Modes of Address. All staff addressed students as 'Miss so and so' at all times, although perhaps in the third year the lecturer in one's special subject might occasionally use one's Christian name. Students always addressed staff formally. (M.H. 1948-51)

I disliked elocution classes but Miss Sadler was an amazing teacher and very precise, and we all found it hard not to laugh when struggling with the likes of:

> *If you saw a pink pug puppy playing ping-pong with a pig or a great, grey goose a-golfing with a goat ... pom pom*
> *Would you think it half as funny as a big, brown Belgian bunny blowing bubbles with a Bishop in a boat!!*

We were taught to notice that when children were absorbed in play they were totally involved and therefore discipline was no problem at all. Learning through play was a phrase constantly used at college. (R.W. 1948-51)

The 1950s: London University Institute of Education

IN her letter to Michaelis Guild members at the start of 1950, Miss Jebb reported:

I suppose I should mention the formal inauguration of the new Institute of Education of London University last month at a ceremony presided over by the Chancellor, the Earl of Athlone, at which the FEI, along with the other twenty-nine Constituent Colleges which form part of the London Institute, was represented by a delegation of staff and students. It marked what I imagine to be a new chapter in the history of the training of teachers, in the bringing together of Colleges and Departments of Education under the protecting aegis of the University.

The language here is interestingly cool: 'I suppose I should…what I imagine to be…'. And was 'the protecting aegis' wishful thinking? Miss Jebb reports in the same paragraph that the Clapham and Streatham Hill Froebel Department was being taken over as a two-year college by the London County Council. Of the five Froebel Colleges in 1945, already two (Bedford was the other) had been taken over by LEAs. Three were left: FEI, Maria Grey, and Rachel McMillan. Two of these were to disappear by 1976.

Miss Jebb argued vigorously at the London Institute of Education, through many committees, to preserve the three-year Froebel training, 'facing opposition with good-humoured inflexibility', as Dr Elsa Walters, Head of Education at FEI, remarked. Her position was not helped by the 1948 Visitation Report, nor by the existence of the Olley 'experiment' with its special two-

year Froebel Certificate programme (which lasted from 1947 to 1953) but, nevertheless, she eventually forced a compromise, so that FEI could retain its three-year course, and students could get a Teacher's Certificate from both the Institute of Education and the National Froebel Foundation. This arrangement applied to entrants from 1950 to 1959 inclusive. Miss Jebb then became a member of the Council of the Institute of Education, and a member of the sub-committee set up to consider the question of a three-year course for all colleges. In 1950 she was made CBE.

Thus began the turbulent and ramshackle mismanagement of teacher education by successive governments in the post-war half-century. Somewhat like the Victorian governess, whose social position was ambiguous ('neither middle class nor working class, neither independent not quite a servant, educated yet propertyless' – Dr John Seed, unpublished MS), teacher training following McNair was not officially regarded as university-type 'education', yet required highly-skilled and educated practitioners. Above all, numbers needed to be controlled in co-ordination with the birth-rate.

The FEI syllabus prior to the 1949 incorporation into the London University Institute of Education had been very practical in its statements. After 1949 there appeared a long preamble which was a statement of a 'General Theory of Education' for all Institute of Education colleges. Its four sections were: 1. General Principles; 2. History of Educational Ideas; 3. Psychology; and 4. Health Education. 'Psychology' is presented as the 'scientific' approach to education. In addition, each student was obliged to take a special subject selected for its value in the personal development of the student, and not necessarily having any connection with his teaching work'. FEI offered Art, Pottery, Textiles, English Literature, Geography, History, Mathematics, Music, Natural History, Religious Knowledge.

The syllabus for 'History of Educational Ideas', while mentioning Montessori and Dewey, fails to mention Froebel, and even in the special College syllabus Froebel is relegated to year three 'when students are better prepared to examine Froebel's principles in the light of modern educational theory and practice'. In 1948 Froebel's two books had been mentioned in the published syllabus, but now he seems to be regarded as belonging to a pre-scientific age. Unlike, apparently, Plato, of whom it is stated, 'a study of Plato's Republic may, where it is thought desirable, serve as a basis for a final reconsideration of educational aims and values'. (In 1963 the name of Froebel was to disappear altogether, even from 'Special Theory of Education'.)

Nevertheless, Miss Jebb was generally positive in outlook during these years in the late 1940s and early 1950s, despite post-war rationing and shortages. These years saw regular rises in teachers' salaries, and the Pelham Scale put women's salaries at the same level as men's. This led to consequential rises in student fees for tuition and residence. Whereas in 1947 tuition and residence had each cost £125 p.a., by 1956 they had gone up to £184 and £159 respectively, rises which affected Froebel students in particular as there was no grant support for the 'extra' first year of study. Further, an increasing number of students were off-campus in approved lodgings for their first year. Nevertheless, recruitment was buoyant – there were 200

applications for 80 places in 1949. (The Bedford Froebel College sadly had only 5 applications for 50 places in the same year, and was taken over by the LEA in 1950.)

Miss Jebb confirmed in a lecture in February 1952, on the 60th anniversary of FEI, the importance of what she called the 'McNair "set up"', and, asserting a continuing connection with the NFF, expressed the hope that 'we shall find increasingly that the texture of our communal life will be strengthened and enriched by the wider setting we now have for our work and social activities'. A non-committal endorsement? A wise and intelligent woman, she doubtless sensed the end of a tradition approaching for the College.

From 1947 and throughout the 1950s, student numbers at Grove House stayed at around 300, with just over 200 resident and about 80 day students. In 1950 it was obvious that day students would be a permanent part of the College's life, rather than an exception, and the Principal and Matron visited a number of landladies in the district and drew up a list of 'approved lodgings' in 1950-51. This was the year that saw the first intake to the course leading to both the Institute of Education Teacher's Certificate and the NFF Teacher's Certificate. When the first cohort were assessed, in 1953, they faced two 3-hour papers set by the Institute of Education on 'Principles of Education', while all other papers, including one on 'Special Theory of Education', were set by NFF. During these years pass rates were good, with about 5% gaining first-class Certificates, and a small number failing, the majority gaining seconds. In 1950 also the role of 'Senior Student' became renamed 'Student President', adopting the university terminology.

Three students with partners at the Jubilee Ball, 1952

'Comus' on the lake, 1952

1952 saw the Jubilee celebrations in recognition of the Foundation of FEI in 1892 and the death of Froebel in 1852. There had been no celebrations in 1942, in the shadow of war. Events included a Garden Party, recitals and exhibitions, and a Service of Thanksgiving at the Friends' Meeting House in Euston Road on a hot afternoon in June. In the same year the gates at the Roehampton Lane entrance, which had been removed for scrap in support of the war effort, were replaced with a pair of gates from an eighteenth-century house in Chiswick. Later that year, as a result of the sale of Offley to Hertfordshire County Council, the 2,700 library books still at Offley (originally brought from Grove House) were written off as part of the sale, and Leonard Montefiore, following in his late father's footsteps, donated 3,300 of his own library books to the college (many of which are now in Templeton). Miss Jebb stated that FEI had the reputation of having the best stocked training college library in the country'. The following

Leonard and Muriel Montefiore at the Jubilee Garden Party, 1952

year caution deposits of five shillings were introduced. (Previously fines for overdue or missing books had been imposed at the end of the year.)

Two very long-serving members of staff died in the mid-1950s, who had been friends to students and influential in their different ways. One was Dorothy Venour, who died in June 1954. She had been a student at FEI from 1919 to 1921, and was Senior Student in the College's first year at Grove House. She became a lecturer in the Nature Department from 1930 to 1945, and when the College returned to Grove House she stayed on as Warden of Offley Training College until 1954. She was a gifted teacher with a warm and selfless personality, and many students paid generous tribute to her. One wrote: 'She exuded a feeling of warmth and safety and home. But it was much more than that. She never wanted you to bend and belong to her. She wanted to set you free to be more wholly yourself'. The other was the Head Gardener, known simply as 'Longhurst', who had been appointed in 1921 when the College moved to Grove House and the thistles had been so thick that you could not see the lake from the terrace. To him was owed the standard of the grounds, to which he was devoted. He died in November 1957, when he was still working on his peach trees and chrysanthemums in the greenhouses (demolished in 1998). Leonard Montefiore wrote, 'Nothing was too much trouble for him. He was almost invariably cheerful, and a chat with Longhurst was something of a tonic'. Miss Jebb recalled that he became something of a Froebelian when 'he came to accept Miss Lulham's view that the "birds were part of the education of the students", so they should be allowed to eat the fruit and gorge on the berries unmolested'. A stone sundial was erected in the grounds in his memory.

During the 1950s the environment of the College changed dramatically from semi-rural to suburban with the building of London's biggest housing scheme of the time, the award-winning high-rise Alton Estate to the south. Also a slice of land to the east was appropriated for the widening of Roehampton Lane. In 1955 Grove House was listed Grade II*, which means 'a building of more than special architectural or historic interest', as one of only six remaining eighteenth-century houses in Roehampton (there had been more than twenty before the LCC's post-war demolition policy).

Miss Jebb in her study, 1955

The retirement of Miss Jebb in 1955 after 23 years was a most significant event for the College. Her previous experience – as Assistant English Tutor at Somerville College, Oxford during World War One, and as lecturer in the Education Department of Birmingham University through the 1920s, with a year as Visiting Lecturer at Wellesley College Massachusetts in 1928-9 – were significant in that she raised the academic standards at the college and radiated an enthusiasm for learning. One writer reflected that 'under her influence the governing body (of FEI) became much more like that of a university college led in its discussions by the principal', and Leonard Montefiore wrote that 'she knew how to get the best out of each member of her staff and of each student. As one of them wrote to her recently, "I never knew that I had it in me, until you showed me that I had"'. Another writer, the long-serving Librarian, Mary Saul, commented that 'she had maintained the liberal spirit of the college', or, as she herself called it, 'the Montefiore tradition'. It was an impressive achievement to have brought the College through the dislocations and relocations of a World War, while continuing to maintain its ethos for ten years thereafter, and to have guided it with its three-year programme intact, into the London Institute of Education. Following her retirement, she was to live for another 23 years, though suffering seriously from arthritis in her later years.

Miss Jebb's successor, Molly Brearley, was, like her, a distinguished, elegant woman with a formidable intellect. Students remember her variously as 'austere, terrifying', 'gentle, warm, welcoming', and 'caustic, tenacious, enlightened'. She was 50 years old on appointment, and had also come from the Education Department of

Birmingham University, where she had worked since 1944. She had a Teacher's Certificate from Liverpool University (she had not taken her degree in English owing to the untimely death of her father), and during the thirties had taught at Kettering Girls' High School. During this period she had become interested in Froebel teaching and had taken the NFU Teacher's Certificate and Trainer's Diploma, which entitled her to work in a Training College. She obtained a post at Bedford Training College, where she worked from 1938 to 1944. She was a researcher in child development, and had supervised postgraduate research at Birmingham, thus enhancing further the academic aspect of the College.

Molly Brearley, 1955

Molly Brearley was to form a very close friendship with Eglantyne Jebb, who became a regular visitor to the College, often staying as guest in the Principal's flat in Grove House. One of Molly Brearley's main tasks was to be the expansion of the College. It was already overcrowded, with nearly 300 students in buildings intended for 20% fewer. Miss Jebb has already commissioned an urgently-needed Physical Education hall, and this was opened in February 1958 by Marie Michaelis, daughter of the first Principal, after whom it was named. It cost £30,000, of which half was paid by the Ministry and half raised by FEI from summer lettings of the College premises during the preceding years. Marie Michaelis died six months after its opening, in August 1958.

Far-reaching social changes also were happening at this time. The coronation of Elizabeth II in 1953 was particularly important in giving an impetus to the cultural dominance of television in coming years (while also marking the end of the radical social policies of the post-war Attlee government). War-time food rationing finally ended in 1954. In 1955 Britain began manufacture of the hydrogen bomb, which was to lead to waves of student protest in the next decade. However, the event which stunned the Western world and caused a massive interrogation and restructuring of education systems was the launching of Sputnik I by the Soviet Union in October 1957, followed by a second satellite in November with a dog aboard, and subsequently the launch of the first manned space capsule with Yuri Gagarin aboard in April 1961. The capitalist West seemed to be falling behind the communist bloc in science and technology in the most dramatic way. Through the twentieth century wars had provided the

impetus for educational change in Britain, as signified by the Education Acts in 1902, 1918, and 1944. Now the Cold War was about to do the same, as education, and the quality of teachers, became supremely important urgent issues.

The last years of the decade were spent in preparation for the new mandatory three-year training course, originally recommended by McNair and due to start in 1960. There would be full integration into Institute of Education syllabuses and examinations, with no separate NFF input. This entailed lengthy discussion and planning, and Molly Brearley wrote, 'We deplore the passing of the Froebel Teacher's Certificate, but we hope to retain all that has made our course valued and known all over the world. We believe that we may still have something unique to contribute to education, in that we never swerve from our conviction that a knowledge of children forms the only safe basis for teaching them. We do not consider this a static affair…'. The conditional mode ('…we believe that we *may* still have something unique to contribute…) is noticeable.

Student Reminiscences from the 1950s

I loved the exploratory course where we had to take something we were bad at at school to know what it was like for a child who had a block and felt he/she could not read. I took art, as at school I had felt a great failure. At my earlier school, we had to draw and get it passed by the teacher before we could paint. Charlotte Stone removed my block by showing me how different artists looked at the world. We visited many art galleries. I learned that I saw negative space more than positive and, using paint to build a picture from the background and seeing shapes within branches, I could practise and depict the objects in the foreground. I still paint in oils and watercolour today. It also helped me understand children with many different learning styles and work with their strengths and weaknesses. (C.H. 1950s)

I believe the year 1952 began with 106 students but we 'lost' about 7 of them on the way, mainly in the first year but two of them in the second year. (One fell from her horse in the vicinity and was killed.) One was 'advised' to leave as she had what was called a 'crush' on the P.E. teacher. (J.M.G. 1952-55)

One or two students had their own cars. Not many of the staff had cars.
In December 1952 there was the famous smog which lasted several days. Even inside it was difficult to see across a room. That was the weekend of the College Ball, and some young men were given permission to sleep overnight on the common room floor.
Nobody smoked or drank as far as I am aware. We didn't think of it. No-one had a radio, as far as I remember, and there was no TV set in college. There were newspapers in the Terrace Room and I used to go there to read the Manchester Guardian, as it then was. Our rooms at college had individual gas meters and 10/- worth of tokens was given to us for our gas fires each term. When we

ran out we had to pay the extra ourselves. We did our weekly washing in the hand-basins in our bedrooms. The clothes were wrung by hand and put into a room heated by hot pipes, and lined with wooden slatted shelves to dry. An iron was available for use in Old Court. I once dried my green college knickers (green to match our college blazers, and the divided skirts in which we did P.E.) on the radiator near the door into Old Court. Miss Shannon (P.E. Lecturer) was not pleased to see them there when she passed by with a man (!) on her way to her room, where I was later called to be reprimanded!
Food was still rationed in 1952 and we had to collect 2 oz. butter each per week for use on our bread and toast. The meal I least liked was Friday (or Saturday?) night's egg curry and mash. I didn't like the curry and had to satisfy my appetite with mashed potato flavoured with tomato ketchup.
I enjoyed Miss Garnett's lectures, and will never forget how she demonstrated the phases of the moon with a globe, an orange and a projector. I had not understood them before. (B.H. 1952-55)

I lived in Old Court in our second year, and in the New Court flat with two other great friends in our third year. I remember the excitement one week when we watched the filming of "Father Brown" in the courtyard below our windows, with Alec Guinness and Olivia De Havilland in the leading roles. (R.R. 1952-55)

In our last week all the tutors gathered with us, and Miss Brearley asked them each to give us a word of advice. I'm afraid I can't remember any except Miss Garnett's, "Know what not to see". On Wednesday evenings there were special lectures or recitals from outside/famous people. Solomon brought his grand piano, well known judges, educationalists and others brought us two hours of great pleasure, stimulation, encouragement, vision or set us thinking.
We took the little boat out on the lake, enjoyed the mallards

coots and moorhens, watched their young swimming around and running for cover. The grounds were beautifully kept and there was always something to stand and wonder at – horse-chestnut trees, leafless in winter, showing off their perfect shape, radiant roses etc..

I should also mention our visits, made in the 3rd year, to Special Schools. It was brilliant to see blind children roller-skating, deaf children being taught to speak. (S.B. 1953-56)

Students were expected to attend all meals and we had to change for dinner (no trousers to this meal though we were allowed to wear them during the daytime). (F.S.M. 1954-56)

I had been educated at a school where academic expectations were high, and Froebel offered an undenominational liberal bias, if this is not a contradiction in terms.

The rigours of Teaching Practice subdued many a free spirit: it was truly a testing time for most students. We learnt how to make classroom equipment because proprietary published or manufactured educational material was in short supply. Schools couldn't afford to let students loose on their precious resources. We learned to be little scavengers of natural and man-made junk, and borrowed pictures and other teaching material from a loan collection at college.

We were very fortunate to be able to attend a series of 'open lectures' held at Grove House by eminent speakers of the day. I can remember hearing Patrick Heron, the artist, Herbert Read, the art historian and critic, A.S. Neill, the founder of Summerhill School, to name but three. (P.D. 1954-57)

Miss Brearley wrote a brief comment on all our final Certificates of Education which indicated our Pass Grade, "Congratulations on a sound Certificate and very best wishes for your new job. Your nearest F.E.I. student who will be very glad to hear from

you is: Miss N. Charlton in Blackheath. Love from M. Brearley". There were no Graduation days – in those days. At the end of each year, the Principal always read out our Reports to us, having each student into her room, individually.

The Danebury Estate was started in my 3rd year – 1957. I remember the horror we all shared as the high-rise buildings began to appear above the trees overlooking Grove House. It was so beautiful before – a wonderful expanse of green – down to Richmond Park.

Roehampton Lane was widened, also in my 3rd year. I had a room in Old Court, looking out on the Lane. In the Autumn Term trees were outside my window – and friendly, old-fashioned lampposts. By the end of the Summer Term, the inevitable transformation had taken place. (K.P. 1954-57)

I was resident at Montefiore – our rooms faced the lake. All the students in the house were foreigners: I was the Nigerian, Yvourne Remedius (who was later my Chief Bridesmaid) was from Jamaica, we had Pigsim from China, Janet Street the Britisher, Juliet Reeve from Kenya, Mattie from India and another girl from Hong Kong. (G.B.O. 1955-58)

Several of my year were "sent down" because they stayed out all night after our summer ball. I have never felt that it was an appropriate decision, because many had parents who were not available to pick them up and they had to find temporary and unsuitable accommodation wherever they could. One of them is now the wife of the former British Consul in Los Angeles. They have just been to stay with me and we shared some laughs about our time at college.

We also got into trouble for this song set to a tune from "Oklahoma":

> I'm just a girl who can't say no
> Froebel's the method for me

I'm just a student working hard
The government's paying my fee
(M.R. 1957-60)

That was the time when a group of girls were "sent down" before the end of term. Their crime was to go to the bowling alley near Heathrow and creep back into their rooms after dawn. Would a fine not have been suitable punishment? But then, it was only just the start of the sixties. (E.M.S. 1957-60)

It was a pretty middle-class establishment then – only one girl from a Secondary Modern in our cohort!
I can't really articulate further about the philosophy since it is an essence as much as anything else which helped us to tune into children and foster creativity, self-esteem and imagination and the will to help children achieve to the best of their ability. I hardly dare to mention the word 'play' and already 'imagination' is a bit of a strong word for today's educational climate. (L.B. 1958-61)

One of my best memories is of badger-watching with a Natural History chum. Out at midnight with torches and sitting up a tree till after 2 a.m. – and oh! the thrill to a London child of seeing my first badger in those college grounds. My friend and I – grandmothers now and still meeting regularly – laugh about that and many other things such as Miss Brearley leading a "prowl" of the grounds on Ball nights to catch "petting" couples!
Socially, spiritually, emotionally it was a complete "growing up" into womanhood. It was summed up by a wise Headmaster many years later when I was applying for a job. "Ah! Froebel College! The Oxford and Cambridge of Training Colleges."
(J.M.D. 1958-61)

I believe that Molly Brearley looked for personal qualities, as well as an enquiring mind. There was a strong sense of principle

which imbued the approach of the college, which I have come to see as its defining characteristic at that time, and one of great value. It endures, and continues to provide inspiration in a way that more superficial training could not do.
Teaching practice was very important. I remember the bus conductor who begged a group of us to warn him when we were to do a lesson on telegraph poles, as we struggled on to his bus early in the morning, laden with all sorts of materials to promote active learning.
The college introduced us to new ideas through a range of lectures on a variety of subjects, given by invited outsiders: I vividly remember E.H. Gombrich talking about perception. I remember too the Socratic dialogues which were the central part of the second-year professional course for the specialist nursery group of students. We had time to reflect on philosophy, morals, the history of education, and it was there that I think the core of principle was imbued into us.
For me, the three years I spent at the college were a necessary time for unforced growth of the spirit as well as of the mind and emotions. I remain profoundly grateful for my time there. The contacts and impressions remain very vivid, and continue to provide a source of energy for what I see as a fight for the hearts and minds of future generations in this era of simplistic measurement and a reductionist, limiting definition of education.
(W.S. 1958-61)

TWELVE

The 1960s: Expansion

SO, in September 1960, 149 students entered the new three-year Certificate course and for the first time had Ministry maintenance grants for each of the three years – provided that they worked in state schools for a designated period of time. The curriculum settled down into a regular pattern, under Institute of Education control. The Exploratory Course continued at one half-day for one term until near the end of the decade, using topics such as toys, waves, the calendar, money, Westminster Abbey, astronomy, stone, crystals, and the law. The Special Subject became renamed 'Main Course' by 1967, and new subjects were introduced: Art of Movement, Drama, and French. Art had expanded to cover Painting, Print & Design, Textiles, Sculpture and Ceramics. During years two and three, students specialised in one of three age-phases: 2-7, 5-9, or 7-11+, and teaching practice was four weeks at the start of term six, and the whole of term seven or eight. Curriculum subjects were taught in years two and in three. There were still College Assemblies weekly on Wednesdays at 1.30 p.m., until numbers grew too large, and they were based on themes explored over a whole term.

Miss Jebb had become Chair of NFF in 1960. Although Molly Brearley insisted in 1960 that 'it cannot be too strongly emphasised that the truly Froebelian character of the course at FEI will remain undiminished', this would be harder to maintain in practice. The last NFF Froebel Teacher's Certificate for FEI students was issued in 1962. It is true that, in addition to teaching practice, students were required to undertake informal contact with children by helping in children's clubs, special schools, and hospitals, as well as being classroom assistants at Ibstock Place and elsewhere. Also the individual tutorial system was

maintained as the basis of teaching, attendance at lectures being 'the student's own responsibility' in years two and three. But these practices were now not uncommon in other colleges. The Froebel three-year training had lasted for 40 years, but was now the rest had caught up and it became harder to sustain what was distinctive in practice about training at FEI, as had been suggested in the Report of the 1948 Institute of Education visitation.

UNIVERSITY OF LONDON INSTITUTE OF EDUCATION

TEACHER'S CERTIFICATE

This is to certify that

Rosemary Lynette Lewis

has completed an approved course of training extending over three years at

Froebel Educational Institute

a Constituent College of the University of London Institute of Education *She* has pursued courses of study and has satisfied the Examiners in the following:

THEORY AND PRACTICE OF EDUCATION, with special reference to the Junior school stage

History   as a Main course   *with Distinction*

She has reached a standard satisfactory to the College in written and spoken English and in a range of subjects, including Mathematics, appropriate to teachers of children at the Junior school stage

9 August 1963.

Curwin Dixon
Secretary

One of the first University of London Teacher's Certificates for three-year trained teachers

In June 1960 there was another regular visitation from the University of London Institute of Education. In a very positive Report it noted that the Governing Body included two University representatives, and that educational policy was formulated at weekly staff meetings. A sign of changing times and values may be discerned in the criticism that staff are spending too much time on tutorial support of students and on school practice supervision: 'We would hope that this generous response to the needs of the students will not prevent members of the staff from continuing their own studies and interests and making available the results to their colleagues and a wider public'. Research and publication will become ever more important as time goes by.

A most revealing statement in the Report is the following: 'The college is perhaps also fortunate in that, up to the present, the fact that students have had to spend the first year as private students without Ministry grant has meant that most have come from more prosperous homes with a good cultural background.' The mystique of the FEI experience had perhaps been as much dependent on the social class and prosperous backgrounds of FEI students (whose parents had been obliged to fund tuition and maintenance fees for the first year) as on the specific teachings of Friedrich Froebel. This is not to diminish the importance and significance of the liberal and child-centred values deriving from Froebel's teachings which were propagated world-wide through FEI graduates. It does explain, however, why FEI seems always to have been regarded as a 'posh' college, even as 'the best' training college.

Now, for the first time, strange as it may seem, the

Government realised that the required supply of teachers was directly related to the birth rate, or, as the National Advisory Council on the Supply and Training of Teachers put it in 1958, 'the Training Colleges had a quantitative relationship to the needs of the schools'. The post-war 'boom' was not diminishing. As the policy objective, since McNair, was to have a fully trained profession, the extra resource of untrained graduates would no longer be available to supplement increased demand.

Nationally there were 20,000 students in training colleges in 1957, mostly on two-year courses. The Advisory Council's 1958 Report predicted that it would be necessary to have 36,000 in training (on three-year courses) by 1962 in order to avoid a national disaster. Five years later, at the time of the Robbins Report (1963), there were 49,000 students in training at 146 colleges, but far from this being regarded as more than enough, the Report recommended that there be 82,000 in 156 colleges by 1970, with a minimum college size of 750 students. Thus, through the 1960s during Molly Brearley's Principalship, the size of the College was to more than double as student numbers inexorably increased:

1959	1960	1961	1962	1963	1964	1965	1966	1967	1968	1969
317	352	383	437	463	479	529	558	635	639	671

Thereafter, through the 1970s, numbers stabilised around the government regulated 'establishment' of 640. This did mean, however, that fundraising for new buildings had become a routine part of College life during the late 1950s and 1960s.

Ministry grants for building programmes were increased from 50% to 75%, and the College responded in 1967

Fundraising: the FEI Christmas Fair in November 1960 was opened by Brian Rix

The Education Block

The Leonard Montefiore Hall & Dining Room

Jebb residences

Leonard Montefiore, c.1960

with the Leonard Montefiore Hall and Dining Room, the Education Block, with four lecture rooms and 13 tutorial rooms (now called 'Cedar'), and Jebb House, with 44 study-bedrooms and a warden's flat (demolished 2000). These were completed, frustratingly behind schedule, and, sadly, Leonard Montefiore died in December 1961 before seeing them complete, the opening being performed by his widow the following May.

Leonard Montefiore had been as committed to FEI as his father had been. He had, like his father, been a student at Balliol (1908-11), where he had absorbed similar ideals of the value of a college environment. He had served in the First War in India and Russia, for which he had been awarded an OBE. Throughout his life he was a passionate advocate of Reform Judaism, arguing that the assimilation of Jews to nations world-wide was preferable to their location in a separate state of Israel. In 1935 he wrote 'Those who stress the racial element in Jewish affairs are merely echoing the opinions of Adolf Hitler'. He worked tirelessly for Jewish refugees throughout the Second War and afterwards. He was never dogmatic about belief. Towards the end of his life he wrote, in a paper called 'What I Believe', 'As for belief, belief is faith chequered by doubts, a chess-board pattern of black and white'.

One obituary stated that 'outside the Jewish community, no institution was closer to his heart than the Froebel Society'. He had been a source of utterly dependable support both to Miss Jebb and to FEI, as Chairman through 22 turbulent years of war and peacetime reconstruction. Though a more private person than his father, he provided a 'ceaseless stream of benefactions' and had a gift for seeing what was comic or amusing in daily incidents. As Miss Jebb was to write, 'It was as a *family friend*' rather than as a Chairman that we enjoyed his presence in our midst. No one was ever so little self-important and so completely simple in his human relationships'. He was, of course, the chief contributor to the College Building Fund. His last message to the College, written to *The Link* a few weeks before his death, included

a warning about the dangers of increasing size, 'of becoming an institution, admirably functional maybe, but where the three years of residence are less memorable than those spent in a smaller but more closely knit unit'. Like his father, he liked to think of FEI in terms of the distinctive character of an Oxford college. Alan Montefiore, son of Leonard, became a Governor of FEI shortly afterwards.

In the same year, 1961, Helen Darbishire, former Principal of Somerville College, Oxford, and Wordsworth scholar, also died. She had been appointed to FEI in 1932, and served until her death. She claimed to be a 'Froebelian at heart, and regarded FEI as 'her second college'.

Joyce Bishop CBE (from 1963 DBE) succeeded Leonard Montefiore in 1961 as Chairperson of FEI. Born in 1896, she had developed a lifelong feminism at Oxford during World War One, and was a strong supporter of married women entering the teaching profession. She had been Headmistress of Godolphin and Latymer School, a Voluntary Aided Girls' Day School in Hammersmith, since 1935 (she retired in 1963), and had been a member of FEI Governing Body since 1951. She also served on numerous national and international committees, including the Association of Headmistresses (of which she had been President), the Governing Body of the Royal Ballet Schools, the University Grants Committee, the Council for Professions Supplementary to Medicine, and UNESCO.

In October 1964, following the election of the Harold Wilson Labour Government, an economic crisis forced a Government moratorium on new building plans. Joyce Bishop wrote in the Annual Report for 1965-66: 'It would be pleasant to be able to report that expansion is

Portrait of Dame Joyce Bishop

going ahead painlessly and that the end of it all is in sight, but alas! we live in a world of squeeze and botching. Plans for building are always cut and the number of students to be admitted is always increased'.

Nevertheless 1967 saw the opening of Garden Court, with 42 study bedrooms, and the Olive Garnett building, which comprised a day students' room and lecture and tutorial rooms, together with the nearby Music rooms (now used by Dance). These buildings were opened on time in July 1967, despite the setback of the builder having been declared bankrupt in January. Olive Garnett had retired in 1965, after a distinguished and record-breaking 39 years on the staff, including spells as Head of Geography and Deputy and Vice-Principal (from 1947 to 1965). She was a nationally distinguished figure in Geography during the period when it was establishing itself as a legitimate academic discipline, and she was a keen advocate of Froebelian principles. Molly Brearley wrote of her that 'she has a freshness of mind about her that is unique'.

The knock-on effects of this intensive building programme included changes of use elsewhere in the College: the former dining room (now the Portrait Room) became a junior common room, and the former assembly hall in Lulham became divided into classrooms for general teaching. In 1966-67 the policy changed with regard to residence: from now onwards first year students had priority, allowing second and third years the freedom to live out in approved lodgings.

This was, of course, the 'sixties', a time when an enormous cultural change was taking place in society at large. The decade had started with the famous lawsuit lifting of the ban on *Lady Chatterly's Lover*, but the Beatles, the pill, hippies, protest movements, and other symptoms of rapid and incremental social change, particularly affecting the young, were leading to seriously reduced respect for traditional authority. The postwar generation was reaching higher education by 1963, and many of the practices and petty rules of the training colleges, about dress, late passes, single-sex residences, etc., were beginning to seem more archaic than ever. As the age of majority was not legally lowered from 21 to 18 until 1968, the College was still officially in *loco parentis.* Nevertheless, student life seemed 'officially' somehow detached from the world outside. The practice of calling students by their titles, e.g. 'Miss Smith', justified as 'that was how they would be referred to in schools', was gradually discontinued at this time. It was not without serious strain that the pedagogic certainties and authority hitherto assumed by the colleges came to be undermined by a more critical and questioning approach.

The domination of teacher-training by unmarried women now began to change slowly. In 1958, out of 35 FEI College staff, 30 were female, and all those were unmarried. By 1971, out of 66 College staff, 29 were male, and of the 37 females 16 were married. One student in 1958 (and several in previous years) 'gave up the course in order to be married'. The first married student (a former nurse with three children) – Barbara Prescott Roberts – was admitted in 1960, when Molly Brearley agreed, on a recommendation from Olive Garnett, to 'let her try'.

The first male students were admitted in 1965, twelve among 517 female students. Twenty-three males were admitted in each of the next two years, and the numbers remained at a similar level until the 1970s. The first

Student Reminiscences from the 1960s

Assemblies had times of silence in the Quaker tradition, which was strange to me coming from a C of E background, but which has been a good experience to have had, for inspecting collective worship in state schools. (M.W. 1961-64)

Froebel was a very friendly place with its excellent system of "godmothers", i.e. second-year students signed up to look after an incoming first year – often someone they knew. It was a very female place with male lecturers and (mature) male students being a rarity. In the end of term assembly (not sure we called it that) Miss Brearley said that "one male had been seen and not heard and another had been heard and not seen" – referring to the devil in "Tobias and the Angel" which I produced and God in "Noye's Fludde" produced by the music department. However, the grant went a long way – I even saved some of mine. We went into London on Saturdays on the bus and for 15 shillings we could take in a matinee from the gods, have a three- course lunch at Lyons Cornerhouse and pay for fares and sweets.
Froebel taught me to be creative, inventive, to plan properly, to see learning through children's eyes and to enjoy learning from children and with them. (S.P. 1962-65)

The values, beliefs and philosophy touched me deeply. The importance of learning through doing – this model of how I would teach was empowering. Many of my peers were critical of those in authority, but I saw them as experienced elders and of great professional stature with whom I could relate, and who seemed to value me without judging me, which was a totally new experience in my life. I felt hugely liberated by being away from home.
My first "shocking" experience was being given an education assignment to read two books (or maybe extended articles) on the

same educational topic which were polarised: presenting me deliberately with conflicting points of view. Like most students, books had, to that date been "true facts", so this was very shocking, and very helpful learning!
I believe that in the era in which I trained, Friedrich Froebel's values were deeply embedded in the more modern academic framework, and in later years when asked to talk to a Montessori student group about Froebel, I realised then how much was implicit in the training. The depth to which I studied Piaget and Bruner and the philosophers gave me a rigorous framework for all future learning. (J.H. 1964-67)

I lived in Templeton and every morning there was a thunderous knock on each bedroom door. The door would then fly open to reveal Miss Airey and her dog. (I think she was assistant Housekeeper.) If by any chance you were still in bed, she would bellow "You ill?" while the dog sniffed under the bed. This poor little terrier was tethered in one of the kitchens for most of the day and shivered when any of us walked by.
On the night of the Ball we could stay out until 1.00 a.m. but no-one was allowed out all night. My first room-mate did just that, arriving back for breakfast in her Ball dress. She was expelled on the spot.
Once a week we had "Rations". We queued outside a storeroom and each student was given a pound bag of sugar, a small tin of coffee or a packet of tea and a jar of jam, chocolate spread or marmalade. I recall one occasion when a friend ate her entire jar of chocolate spread that evening, licking it off a knife!
We were all in awe of the Principal and aghast to hear that she had caught two students, on the roof of Main House, sunbathing topless. She lectured them about health risks and sent them in!
I could recount a number of horror stories – the student, with boyfriend, caught by the police on the fire escape, trying to climb in – the fellow student who locked herself in the stock cupboard

on teaching practice and refused to come out – and, of course, PE endured, in mixed groups, whilst still having to wear those dreadful green interlock knickers! (R.W. 1966-69)

I was a mature student (43 when I started), and on entering the grounds for the first time I was amazed and delighted to see a whole lot of young ladies crawling around in the grass with magnifying glasses, bottoms in the air and obviously exploring nature. I thought that any college that could get students doing this must, indeed, be special!
Unfortunately it was during these years that the staff were put under pressure to get further degrees in order not to be made redundant. There was a noticeable unease among them, which filtered through to the students. (N.V. 1969-72)

married male student who was also a parent was admitted in 1967. (After a period as Dean of Education and Professor of Music Education at Roehampton Institute, this former student, Graham Welch, went on in 2001 to take up an appointment as Professor of Education at the University of London Institute of Education.) However, men have always been in a minority at the College even after diversification of the curriculum in the 1970s, as the college has continued to maintain a specialism in primary teacher education, which mainly attracts female students.

The period from 1963 to 1971 may be considered the period of Education Reports, each of which affected the College to a greater or lesser extent. The Newsom Report (August 1963), entitled 'Half our Future', was concerned with the quality of secondary modern schools. It recommended that all graduates wishing to enter teaching should be trained, and that the training colleges (as opposed to university departments of

education) would be the most suitable places to undertake this as they offered a concurrent training (personal higher education with pedagogical studies).

The Robbins Report on Higher Education (October 1963) was a signal for expansion of higher education. It recommended establishment of six new universities, the upgrading of CATs (Colleges of Advanced Technology) to university status, the establishment of polytechnics, and of a national degree-awarding body (CNAA). It also renamed training colleges 'Colleges of Education', stipulated that they should have independent governing bodies, and recommended that they be permitted to offer a four-year degree (the BEd), which would provide parity with the degree-plus-PGCE training route. In 1966, Anthony Crosland, Secretary of State for Education, in his famous Woolwich speech referred to the polytechnics along with colleges of education, as part of 'the public sector', as distinct from 'the autonomous sector', meaning the universities. Though the Ministry rhetoric in 1958 in introducing the three-year training courses for teachers had been of fostering 'an academic and social life in the colleges more akin to that in universities', the overwhelming imperative was the Ministry's need to control the colleges' numbers and finances more or less directly. This was now the primary obstacle preventing them from entering the privileged 'autonomous' sector.

The concise Weaver Report (1966) made recommendations on the governance of colleges of education. It agreed that 'the Secretary of State, in determining a national policy for the supply of teachers, must be enabled to control the number of colleges and their individual size and character'. It required both maintained and voluntary colleges to establish governing bodies, and stipulated their powers and, in outline, their composition, i.e. to include representatives from the associated university, academic staff, local teachers, and others. The Report also required the establishment of college Academic Boards, which were to include representatives from each subject department and from elected staff and students. These requirements were to ensure the reconciliation 'of academic freedom with social responsibility', and were introduced with particular reference to LEA colleges, which were often directly controlled by the Local Education Committee.

The effects on FEI were fundamental. The College name officially changed in 1964 to 'The Froebel Educational Institute College of Education'. In 1969 FEI formulated a new constitution which established a separate Governing Body for the College 'of no more than 20 persons', as stipulated by legislation, with delegated powers from the renamed FEI 'Council of Management'. (Actually, what seems to have happened at this point was that the FEI Governing Body declared itself the Governing Body of the College, and selected half of its membership to be the FEI Council of Management.) One big innovation was that for the first time two students, the President and Vice-President of the Students' Union, were officially members of the College Governing Body.

In 1967, following the Robbins recommendation, the first BEd programme was offered at FEI, and in that year 18 third-year students qualified to continue to the fourth year. (They were required to have an overall academic profile in their Certificate studies of at least 'B' standard, with at least 'C' in practical teaching.) Of those only 12 chose to stay on, and, one year later, nine

graduated, one was classified Upper Second, five Lower Second, and three Pass. For ten years this was the general picture: about 10% of Certificate entrants qualified for and took the BEd. There were no Firsts until 1975, when Alison Reddish was awarded one. Thereafter, following diversification, the proportion increased rapidly to about 5%.

Molly Brearley had been appointed in 1963 as a member of the Committee chaired by Lady Plowden to investigate and make proposals on primary education, and had been actively working on its behalf until the publication of the Report in 1967. This was a generation after the Hadow Report, which, in 1933, had advocated Froebelian methods and endorsed the NFF Teacher's Certificate as an appropriate qualification. The Plowden Report was entitled 'Children and their Primary Schools' and was described at the time as 'thorough, humane and liberal' in the *Guardian*. In retrospect it can be seen as the high point of the progressive movement in education. Membership of the Committee had included intellectuals, such as A.J.Ayer and Michael Young, as well as educators, such as Molly Brearley, and others. The Committee visited many schools and colleges, including FEI, and received many submissions, including one from the NFF. The Report began with the words, 'At the heart of the educational process lies the child', and its child-centredness resonated forcefully with Froebelian values and practices. It denounced corporal punishment and rote learning, and emphasised the importance of systematic nursery education, parent participation, and the concept of 'learning-readiness'. It also proposed the establishment of Educational Priority Areas, in which more money and resources would be devoted to areas of social deprivation.

Molly Brearley on Grove House Terrace in 1967, on publication of the Plowden Report

Lady Plowden herself, one of the last embodiments of that enduring British caste of 'the great and the good' whose members had chaired national bodies and commissions for social reform in a relatively non-partisan way, felt strongly that the national interest was dependent on a sound education system (as did Froebel). She wrote, five years later that 'much of the misunderstanding and violence in society … comes from a deep feeling of isolation and injustice ingrained in our city failures and within our education system'. The Report was rightly attacked by sociologists at the Institute of Education, led by Professor Basil Bernstein, for its serious lack of sociological analysis. However, what came to be called 'Plowdenism' – a caricature of the carefully nuanced Report – soon generated a new right within education, led by Professor Brian Cox of Manchester University, and articulated in the infamous 'Black Papers'. The backlash against Plowden and child-centred methods is still deeply embedded in official policy.

Molly Brearley had been academically active throughout her period of office as Principal. Her last substantial publications as Principal were *A Teacher's Guide to Reading Piaget* (with Elizabeth Hitchfield) in 1966, and *Fundamentals in the First School,* an edited collection of papers by College staff, in 1969. (She followed this with *Educating Teachers* in 1972.) She must have felt very proud to have participated in the production of the Plowden Report, which so unambiguously validated Froebelian practice. At last national recognition for the values and practices advocated by FEI had been achieved after just 75 years! But already the dark clouds had gathered. The last Froebel Teacher's Certificates had been awarded by NFF in 1962, and the organisation was struggling to survive. Repeated requests were made for ex-students to join. (It finally ceased to exist in November 1975.) Relations with Ibstock Place, still called 'The Demonstration School' in 1967, but not thereafter, began to change, as the College's attention was necessarily turned towards the Institute of Education and the DES.

In the 1967 issue of *The Link*, the annual journal of the Michaelis Guild, Eglantyne Jebb and Molly Brearley wrote a joint letter in 'an attempt to survey the past history of FEI and to make some suggestions as to its future'. In fact there were no suggestions as to the future, merely an expression of regret at 'a certain loss of the intimacies only possible in a small community', with an uncertain 'but may we not also hope that more and more students will go out from the College in a pioneering spirit –ready to experiment with new teaching techniques…?'. In the same 1967 issue of *The Link,* however, were 20 pages of 'News of Guild Members Overseas', following up a similar article in the 1965 edition. On every continent, in scores of commonwealth and non-commonwealth countries, former FEI students were working or living or retired, and were in touch with the Guild. Many students also had been for many years recruited from overseas, given the world-wide spread of the reputation of Froebelian training. This really was living testimony to the international nature of the Froebel movement, and the commitment of its members to its values. It had begun as an international movement, and remains so to this day.

Mention must be made at this time of an FEI lecturer in Education who was to become the foremost British Froebel scholar of the next three decades, Joachim Liebschner. A German national by birth, his first

Joachim Liebschner, May 2001

experience of Britain was as a prisoner of war. He trained as a teacher in England, and then, after secondment to Froebel College on a Diploma course, became a committed Froebelian – so much so that, having left the staff of FEI in 1966 to take up a post at another college, he returned two years later to FEI. He was conducting original research, and in 1968, despite eastern bloc restrictions, located original Froebel manuscripts and letters in Dresden and in the archives of the University of Sciences, East Berlin. Joachim Liebschner's continuing scholarly work led to numerous courses and lectures during the 1970s and 1980s, at FEI and abroad, and in particular resulted in the publication of two important books, *Foundations of Progressive Education: the History of the National Froebel Society* (1991), and *A Child's Work: Freedom and Play in Froebel's Educational Theory and Practice* (1992).

THIRTEEN

The 1970s: The End of Independence – Roehampton Institute of Higher Education

MOLLY Brearley retired in 1970, only the fourth FEI College Principal in nearly 80 years. All had been powerful and distinguished women. At the time of her appointment, Leonard Montefiore had stated that Molly Brearley 'has a formidable task in continuing the Lawrence-Jebb tradition'. She continued it with distinction, personally and nationally, uninhibited by the ever-present shadow of Miss Jebb, who had continued to submit an annual letter to *The Link*, along with Molly Brearley's, every year up to 1970. They continued indeed, at the request of the Guild, to contribute right up to 1977, Jebb missing only years 1971-73. Molly Brearley had written in 1957 in one of these letters, 'But no one, I find, ever leaves the FEI!'. She became President of the Guild on her retirement, at which time there were about 1500 members.

Priscilla Steele with a group of students

The new Principal was Priscilla Steele. She had been Principal of Darlington College of Education since January 1962, and had steered that college through its period of expansion. She had originally trained at the Bedford Training College, and taken a Diploma in the Psychology of Childhood at Birmingham University and an MEd at Manchester University. After some years of school teaching, she had become a lecturer and subsequently Head of Education at the Manchester Day Training College, from where she moved to Darlington as Principal.

The Lawrence-Jebb-Brearley tradition was an enormous burden for the new Principal to carry, and it was eventually to put an unsustainable pressure on her. During her first year at FEI a new building was erected for the Students' Union, and it was called the Brearley Building. Although after one year, Dame Joyce Bishop wrote that Priscilla Steele had, 'by her unerring perception, her imaginative understanding and her vigorous participation become so completely involved in [the life of FEI] that she is already an integral part of it', events were to indicate otherwise, despite her personal qualities.

1970 proved to be a fateful year for Colleges of Education, and was to signal the beginning of the end. Within five years they would disappear. In June 1970 the DES convened a conference of Principals of Colleges of Education in York. It had noticed that the birth rate had dropped significantly in the previous few years, and so the expansion of teacher education proposed by Robbins was now to be put in reverse. Colleges would have to transfer resources from initial to inservice training, and a series of aggressive questions was posed by DES Under

Secretary Hugh Harding, in challenging the existence of monotechnic teacher training institutions: 'If monotechnics are bad are polytechnics good?…Would development of liberal arts colleges weaken professional education?…Is there a case for some colleges withdrawing from teacher education?'

Hugh Harding would prove to be a powerful and ruthless operator at the DES. During four years in the mid-1970s there would be no fewer than four Secretaries of State for Education (Margaret Thatcher, Reg Prentice, Fred Mulley, and Shirley Williams) and four Ministers of State for Higher Education (Norman St John-Stevas, Gerry Fowler, Lord Crowther-Hunt and Gordon Oakes), thus enabling Harding to consolidate his power and control. Not one of these politicians attempted to formulate a clear strategy for teacher training, and thus 'policy' in this period was to become the total of individual decisions masterminded by Harding, ostensibly as 'advice' from the DES.

In December 1970 Secretary of State Margaret Thatcher appointed a small Committee of seven people, chaired by Lord James, Vice-Chancellor of the University of York, to report speedily on the content and structure of teacher education, and the roles of colleges, polytechnics and universities in it. By April 1971 the Committee was drafting its Report – the James Report. It was published in November 1971, and entitled 'Teacher Education and Training'. Speculation had been rife about its proposals during the previous year – the 'waiting-for-James' period. In the event it proposed the severing of colleges' links with university schools of education, and recommended three sequential 'cycles' of education and training for

teachers: personal education, pre-service training and in-service training, this last to be expanded as a matter of priority. The colleges should require 2 A-level entry and offer 3-year degree courses and a 2-year DipHE.

DES officials advised the Principals of the colleges in south-west London, that any institution with fewer than 2,000 students would be in future non-viable, and that some grouping of colleges in the area would be strongly advised. Thus it came about that, on 28 June 1972, a historic meeting between the Principals of the four

Lewis Howdle, who was between 1972 and 1978 in sequence Vice-Principal, Acting Principal, and Deputy Principal

voluntary colleges in south-west London took place at FEI, to discuss how they might co-operate. The colleges were all located within two miles of each other – Froebel Institute College, Digby Stuart College next door in Roehampton (Sacred Heart foundation), Southlands College in Wimbledon (Methodist foundation) and Whitelands College in Putney (Anglican foundation). The issue now for FEI was not about survival of Froebelian values and practice in the College, but survival *tout court*.

The pressures of the present, together with the burden of the College tradition, put a strain on the new Principal which she was not able to withstand. In the autumn of 1972 she went on long-term sick leave, and the Chair of Governors, Dame Joyce Bishop, appointed Lewis Howdle (Deputy Principal) together with three senior

Education:

A Framework for Expansion

Presented to Parliament by the Secretary of State for Education and Science
by Command of Her Majesty
December 1972

LONDON
HER MAJESTY'S STATIONERY OFFICE

31½ p

The title-page of the White Paper which led to the dissolution of the Colleges of Education. 'The Government intend that...some colleges either singly or jointly should develop as major institutions....concentrating on the arts and human sciences.'

members of staff (called the 'Junta') to stand in for her for the year. She resigned in August 1973 to take up a post as General Inspector with Birmingham Local Education Authority.

December 1972 saw the publication of the White Paper, *Education: a Framework for Expansion* (commonly called at the time a 'frame-up for contraction'), which confirmed Government acceptance of most of the James Report recommendations, with the major exception that there would be no coherent 'third sector' of teacher training institutions. Rather the college facilities would be used to expand general public higher education outside the universities. There were already 114,000 students in training in 1972 (a 40% increase on the Robbins recommendation): the White Paper revealed that a maximum of only 70,000 places would be needed by 1981, and stated unambiguously:

> *Some colleges must face the possibility that in due course they will have to be converted to new purposes; some may need to close...the substantial broadening of function proposed for the great majority of the colleges of education will involve their much closer assimilation into the rest of the non-university sector of higher and further education. Put another way, a college which expands and diversifies, either alone or by joining forces with a sister college...will not be easily distinguishable by function from a polytechnic...'*

On 28 March 1973, DES Circular 7/73, *Development of Higher Education in the Non-University Sector* was published. It announced an expansion of non-teacher-training HE places, mostly in the polytechnics, and

Dame Joyce Bishop talking in 1984 with Leslie Morris (College Vice-Principal, 1969-72)

and to strengthen its links with the university by seeking its sponsorship of existing degree courses and for those it is hoped to initiate in combined studies to degree level.

Meanwhile talks between the Colleges had continued through 1972-73, and alternative partners or possibilities had also been considered. These included: a federation to include local LEA colleges (Battersea and Garnett Colleges in Roehampton, Philippa Fawcett in Streatham, and Furzedown in Tooting), a federation to include Chelsea College (a college of the University of London), and, in the case of FEI, a relocation to Suffolk, where the Local Education Authority had no teacher training provision and wished to attract a college to its area.

Dr Eric Briault, the Education Officer of the Inner London Education Authority (ILEA), having consulted widely, produced his proposals in October 1973. Hugh Harding had made known the view of the DES that any federation in south-west London should be strongly centralised, if not a complete merger. Dr Briault took this line in his recommendations. He wrote:

My proposal for these four colleges (Southlands, Whitelands, Digby Stuart and Froebel) was that they should form a federation in South-West London, with a total of about 3,130 students. My definition of a federation involves, among other features, a strong centralised body having control of the resources of the federation. [This] would have an excellent chance of providing an organisation within which colleges could retain their own identity [and also provide] an excellent range of options for non-teacher courses.

asked Local Education Authorities to submit plans for their areas, to include (controversially) voluntary Colleges of Education. It was on the same day that the Senate of London University approved the introduction of a 3-year BEd degree without honours, and agreed to co-operate in the diversification of courses at the colleges associated with its Institute of Education. The DES arranged another conference for Principals at Oxford in April, which was opened by Margaret Thatcher herself, to discuss the implications for the future of colleges – in fact, their dissolution.

Dame Joyce Bishop wrote of the 1972-73 academic year:

Never can there have been so many meetings of the providing body of the FEI as have been held during this academic year – all concerned with change…It is our firm intention to discover ways of preserving the independence of the College and its particular excellence which is recognised both nationally and internationally

The following month, on 28 November 1973, a meeting took place at Whitelands of the Principals and Chairs of Governors of the four colleges, at which a Statement of Intent was drawn up for delivery to the DES. This was a significant achievement. It stated that 'the four colleges now declare that it is their intention actively to pursue discussions to establish and Association of their four Colleges'. It stated the intention to offer BEd and other degrees of the University of London, including higher degrees, and to set up a joint planning body to provide a 'unified channel of communication' with the DES. It confirmed the intention to establish a Formation Committee, under an experienced and independent chairman, and, in due course, to propose a 'constitutional instrument' for the Association 'which would not be incompatible with the retention of the autonomy of the four colleges'. Thus the struggle between centralisation and college autonomy began, a struggle which would last indefinitely.

At first there was a great deal of resistance to the Roehampton 'association' by staff and Governors alike, but by 1975, when the fate of the other 160+ former Colleges of Education was becoming known, this attitude perceptibly changed. Most were to be 'swept away in the tornado of change', as Dame Joyce Bishop succinctly put it. (The local LEA colleges were all to close soon afterwards.) Nevertheless, there still remained strong reservations about the possible practical implications.

Early in December 1973 the University of London issued guidelines for new diversified degree awards in its colleges, requiring outline syllabuses and course structures to be submitted within little more than a month, by 18 January 1974. The Formation Committee met for the first time on 9 January 1974. It was agreed that membership would be the Principals, two Governors and two Academic Board members of each of the four colleges, and that an external Chair should be

Professor James Topping, Chairman of the RIHE Formation Committee

sought. By the third meeting Dr James Topping, recently retired vice-chancellor of Brunel University, had been invited to become chairman, a role which he ably fulfilled. He was immensely experienced in relevant areas, having guided the transformation of Brunel from technical college to university. While sympathetic to the position of the colleges, he was a realist, calm and balanced but firm of purpose, a clear thinker and a skilled and patient negotiator. The constitutional framework which was eventually produced owed more to him than to any other person.

The Formation Committee agreed that the proposed new institution would be called the Roehampton Institute of Higher Education. The successor body to the Formation Committee would be, in 1975, the RIHE Council. Each college was determined to preserve its identity as far as possible, so a merger was ruled out. At its second meeting it established a Joint Interim Academic Planning Body, or JIAPB (pronounced 'Jap'). This would eventually become the RIHE Senate, and it was also chaired by Dr Topping. He continued to chair both bodies until December 1978.

The JIAPB would be responsible for making recommendations on academic policy and, in particular, for negotiating the new, diversified courses of study with the London University Institute of Education, so that they could be offered to students for the target entry date of 1975. Institute of Education rules meant that they would have to be two-subject 'unit-based' degrees (a form of primitive modularity). Also, a new degree title, in addition to BA and BSc, would need to be adopted and approved – the BH (Bachelor of Humanities) for those subjects which the University of London did not offer internally.

While these intensely important discussions were taking place during 1973-74, the FEI College was without a Principal. Lewis Howdle was made Acting Principal for the year while the post of Principal was advertised, a role which he fulfilled effectively, with conscientious commitment.

Michael Morgan

It needed a brave person indeed to take on the principalship of a College which was not only in the throes of negotiating an uncertain future, but one that had also been without a Principal effectively for nearly two years. Michael Morgan was appointed. He had been a lecturer at Bognor Regis College of Education, and became not only the first male Principal of the College, but also the first married Principal. He proved to be a dynamic defender and representative of the College.

The proposed new Constitution of RIHE was presented to Hugh Harding at the DES in June 1974. His response in a letter of 27 June was highly critical, stating that 'as conceived, the Institute seems to us to be much more like [a] loose association of colleges...than [a] strong federation'. Meanwhile there was a General Election in October 1974 and the return of a Labour Government. Nevertheless, in a further letter as late as 9 January 1975 Hugh Harding was writing 'I am bound to say I am disappointed that subsequent consideration has led to so little change. It is not a document which I could recommend to Ministers in its present form'. This led to further correspondence and a meeting with Dr Topping. Finally agreement was reached on staffing (all staff except Principal, Deputy Principal and Bursar must be employed centrally by the Institute), on withdrawal (colleges could withdraw from the Institute either in 1980-82 or in 1996-97, but not thereafter), and on other matters, including the institution of redundancy procedures (Harding expected about 25% of staff to be declared redundant in due course).

It was eventually, on 9 July 1975, that Fred Mulley, the new Labour Government's Secretary of State for Education, approved the establishment of the federal Roehampton Institute of Higher Education 'as a major new initiative in the field of higher and further education'. Its first students entered in that September. The formal legal agreements were not, however, signed until more than three years later. Formal approval had to

Froebel College in 1975

be gained from four governing bodies, four providing bodies, and from the Charity Commissioners. It was not until 30 November 1978 that all necessary approvals were in place, and each of the colleges became signatory to the Declaration of Trust, with associated Instrument and Articles of Government, which established the Institute in law, and a 'Deed of Adherence' to RIHE, involving a transfer of the control and maintenance of their assets within defined limits. Here was a foretaste of the complexity that would frustrate decision-making in the newly-formed Institute.

Strong leadership was required to take the College forward while preserving its 'ethos'. This word was used so much that it became almost a joke among staff, but it went with a total proscription of words such as 'merger', 'amalgamation', and 'sites' ('campuses' was the correct usage). In addition to the Principal and Deputy Principal, this leadership was provided by some senior Froebel staff

Alan Montefiore talking to Kevin Keohane, late 1970s

Chairman of the FEI Council of Management and also as Chairman of the College Governors, posts which he held with distinction until 1979. Michael Morgan later recorded that Alan Montefiore had been 'the major architect of the creation of this unique federal Institute at Roehampton'. He remained on the FEI Council for some years.

An enormous publicity campaign had been launched by the College and by Roehampton Institute (the 'of Higher Education' was increasingly dropped). It was desperately important that the colleges and the new Institute should advertise themselves. They needed to use all means available to recruit to totally new degree programmes that nobody knew about (they were not even approved by the University until the summer of 1975), and to an institution that nobody had heard of, and even to a new degree, the BH, that nobody understood. Teacher training entrants to Froebel were restricted to 95 in 1976 and to 55 in 1977, a 75% cut on ten years earlier. In November 1977, the Government estimated the number of training places required by 1981 to be only 4,000.

who were promoted in Michael Morgan's first term and later became prominent in RIHE. These included Audrey Coe (Dean of Studies), Mollie Davies (Dean of Students), and Sheila Roberts (Senior Tutor). Sheila Roberts, a committed Froebelian and gifted Mathematics tutor, was elected Deputy Principal on a three-year term in 1978. This was subsequently extended by one year, when, on retirement in 1982, she became Chair of Governors of Ibstock Place School for three years.

In 1975, Alan Montefiore, the distinguished philosopher and son of Leonard, took over from Dame Joyce Bishop as

The figures show the success of the efforts made at Froebel to diversify recruitment away from initial teacher education, following a strategy devised and led with spirited determination by Michael Morgan. (One aspect of this was that all staff were required to give presentations and distribute publicity material at all secondary schools that they knew, including those at which they had been pupils – in some cases several decades previously.) The advertising and recruitment drive was a big success: total College numbers held up to target throughout this period of turbulent change, at about 650, and RIHE survived.

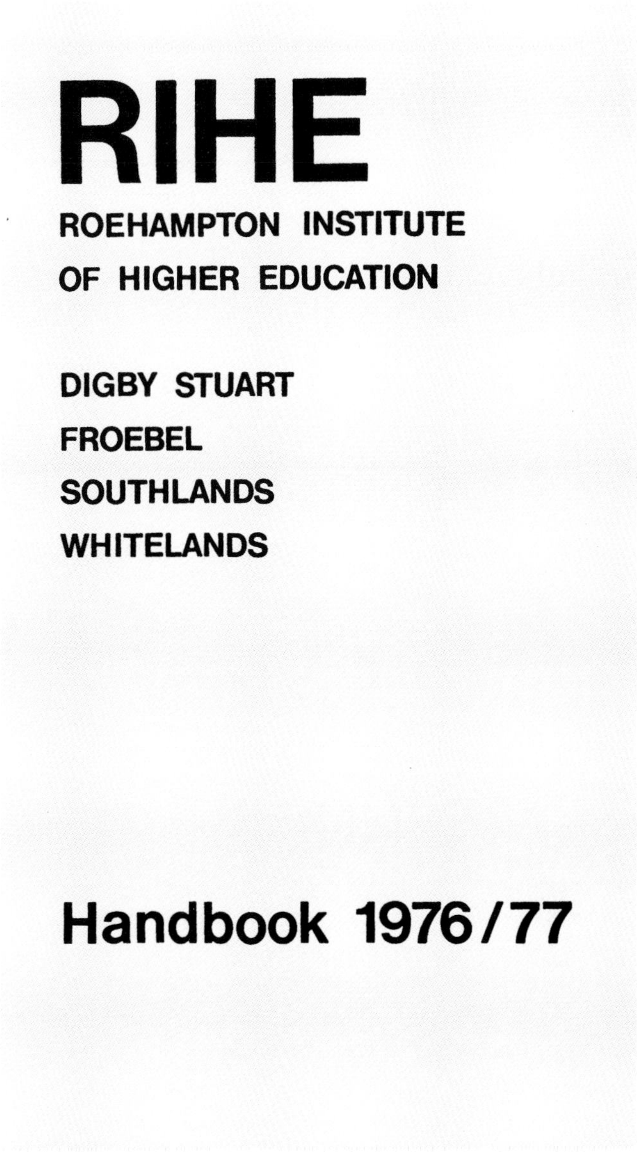

RIHE

ROEHAMPTON INSTITUTE OF HIGHER EDUCATION

DIGBY STUART
FROEBEL
SOUTHLANDS
WHITELANDS

Handbook 1976/77

The first RIHE Prospectus

	1975	1976	1977	1978	1979
BEd	66	74	48	58	52
Certificate	97	51	14	–	–
BA(Combined)	13	42	70	68	82
BH(Combined)		33	50	47	62
BSc(Combined)			1	12	7

An important feature of the diversification drive was the introduction of higher degrees. A new Masters degree in Education had been validated in 1974, and another in Music Education in 1975, which between them recruited fairly steadily about 12-15 students each year, about half being part-time. Within twenty years there would be more than 30 Masters degree programmes.

The new Institute was by some regarded as 'the Goldsmiths College of south-west London'. Perhaps the DES assumed that merger would follow in due course. There was to be no extra money for the collegiate structure (despite the Oxbridge precedent), and the federation would be entirely centrally funded, with internal allocation to the colleges. At first, a common view among staff was that the colleges would carry on much as before but with new degree programmes and an extra 'dimension' deriving from co-operation, where appropriate, with the other colleges. An enormous amount was to depend on the person appointed to lead this complex organisation. It was agreed that an external appointment was needed, and the post of 'Rector' was advertised in late 1975.

The successful candidate at interview on 26 January 1976 was Dr Kevin Keohane CBE, Vice-Principal and Director of Science Education at Chelsea College, University of

Dr Kevin Keohane at Froebel

London. He took up his appointment in the summer of 1976. He was a physicist, and had been Director of the highly-acclaimed Nuffield Primary Science Project in the 1960s. His supreme political virtues were affability and patience with interminable negotiation. He was a man of vision and energy, intolerant of woolly thinking, self-importance or obfuscation, who encouraged high academic aspiration, and even in those unpropitious times saw Roehampton as a potential university. An educator himself, he was to oversee massive cuts in teacher training at his new institution, a major programme of staff redundancy, and the introduction of a totally new unit-based curricular structure. His major achievement, to which the College and RIHE owed their very survival, was keeping the four providing bodies talking and working together. Throughout his period of office (to 1988), as compromises were required, it was a constant possibility that one or all would decide to withdraw their assets, sell the college, and devote the resources to other purposes. While some staff remained resolutely loyal to memories of the former college times, others cared more for the development of their academic subject, now that the majority of students were not training to be teachers, and preferred to belong to a unitary Institute. Kevin Keohane had to see both sides of the issue, and encourage loyalty from the colleges, as well as the strenuous academic development which only the Institute could promote.

FEI had built a new detached house for its new Principal, as Michael Morgan was the first Principal with a family, so it offered the Principal's flat in Grove House as accommodation for the central administration of RIHE. This became the Rector's office until 1985, when part of the Sacred Heart convent next door was leased for £325,000 and refurbished for use as the RIHE Senate House.

A major priority now was academic organisation. RIHE comprised about 3,000 students and about 300 staff in 1976. Each college had its own departments, with their own heads, so there were four departments of Education, for example, and four departments of Art, English, etc.. The Formation Committee and JIAPB had introduced the temporary expedient of 'syndicates', with elected fixed-term Chairs. This was clearly not sustainable, and in 1979-80 Kevin Keohane introduced a programme of appointing permanent Heads to the joint academic departments following national advertisement. This was simultaneous with a redundancy programme, which was very stressful (though the terms offered under 'Crombie' were relatively generous). A rapid worsening of student-staff ratios in the early 1980s, in conjunction with the necessity to make appointments of new staff with expertise relevant to the new degree programmes, made this period particularly difficult. It was hard, after years of loyal service to teacher training, for more mature members of staff to see themselves 'replaced' by new young academics with little knowledge of or concern for the history of the colleges or teacher training.

Molly Brearley, from her semi-retirement (she was still external examiner in more than ten institutions in 1977)

wrote, understandably, with bitterness about the changes in teacher education. 'Words fail me…I have found very many unhappy staff members who are trying to make something good out of very fragmented and disturbed courses…the bureaucrats get away with too much if you don't watch out.' A very sad event followed in 1978, with the death of Eglantyne Jebb at the age of 88.

Meanwhile developments in the College continued under Michael Morgan's direction, two of which deserve particular note. In 1975 the College Social Club and Bar was opened, in the former kitchen-then-sculpture-room adjacent to the students' common room (now the Portrait Room, and a lecture room since 1995). It was to remain there until 1996. Then, in 1977, the Early Childhood Archive was established, with support from the Manpower Services Commission, and based upon a substantial part of the NFF Archive, which had moved to Grove House in 1971, together with items donated by Joachim Liebschner and others. It is now on the top floor of Grove House, and is called the 'Froebel Archive for Childhood Studies'. It is a major resource for researchers world-wide, and details of its literature contents are accessible online through the University of Surrey Roehampton website.

In April 1979, all teaching staff were transferred to the payroll of RIHE, following the signing of the formal legal establishment of RIHE the previous November, and Gerald East succeeded Alan Montefiore as Chair of the FEI Council of Management and of the College Governors that summer.

The Constitution of FEI now was revised. In 1981 a 'Memorandum of Association' established the FEI

Gerald East

Rory Hands

As if all that change were not enough, the decade ended with the momentous decision by the University of London to cease validation of courses in former colleges of education. This decision, by a committee chaired by Lord Annan, took place while the quinquennial revalidation of courses was taking place in the Institute. The DES expected RIHE, in common with several other colleges, to submit themselves for validation by the Council for National Academic Awards (CNAA), the body which validated degree programmes in polytechnics. However, Kevin Keohane, ever visionary, and realising the potential sizeable academic asset that RIHE represented, made an informal approach to the University of Surrey, 22 miles down the A3 at Guildford. Surrey was a technological university (formerly the Battersea College of Advanced Technology which had been established as Battersea Polytechnic in 1891, the year before FEI), and had no significant provision of arts or humanities subjects, and no initial teacher education, and so it might be considered to be an ideal complementary partner with RIHE. The University could gain significant income from validation fees, and through RIHE could offer the Surrey degree over a wider range of subjects.

Council, analogous to a Board of Directors, which would work through three 'committees of the Council', i.e. College Governing Body, School Governing Body, and Froebel Research Committee. The 'Froebel Association' would be analogous to shareholders, but without any financial requirement. The School now had a Governing Body for the first time. For the College, Rory Hands, a distinguished and cultured former headmaster, who had been a College Governor since 1972, became Chairman of the College Governing Body, while Gerald East continued as Chair of Froebel Council. This was the first time that the two positions had been held by different people. Rory Hands, a sceptic about RIHE, was to serve in this role for ten years, until 1989, when he became Chairman of FEI Council, succeeding Gerald East, until 1993. Many of the College's valuable assets – paintings and porcelain – were sold at this time by FEI, supposedly because of a fear of burglaries.

FOURTEEN

Transition: into University of Surrey Roehampton

A group of Froebel staff in 1982, just before the first student entry to University of Surrey award programmes at RIHE. Several of those pictured were to become Deans, Professors, Heads of School or to take up other promoted posts in the University of Surrey Roehampton twenty years later.

AND so it happened. The Senate of the University of Surrey met on 29 January 1980 to consider the RIHE request for validation of its courses, on the same day as the RIHE Senate was meeting. The result was anxiously awaited, but no news came until the next day. The decision was positive. A committee called the 'Delegacy' was established to control relations with RIHE, and later with other associated institutions of the University. The first Chairman was Professor Terence Lee, who had been a strong advocate within the University of establishing links with RIHE. Following validation visits organised by the University of Surrey through 1980-81, the first students were admitted to University of Surrey award programmes in 1982. The first 34 Surrey PGCE awards were conferred on Froebel-assigned RIHE students in 1983, a further 29 in 1984, and 1985 witnessed 83 BA (Joint Honours) awards, 40 BSc (Joint Honours) awards, a further 34 PGCE awards, and one MA in Education. The other RIHE colleges showed a similar pattern.

Jill Redford, seventh Principal of Froebel College

Following the appointment of Heads of Departments in 1979-80, the vexed question arose of departmental location. Should a college staff include representatives of all the subjects offered by RIHE? Or should each department be located in only one of the colleges, in the interests of departmental coherence and academic development? For a time there was an uneasy compromise, with staff being 'assigned' to one college (on the demand of the Principal) but often 'located' in another. Eventually the academic imperative was victorious over the college demands, and Senate agreed in May 1982, following discussion of a strongly-argued paper from the Rector, that 'as a matter of policy, steps should be taken towards centralisation of departmental teaching and resources'. It was a particularly acute question in the practical subjects because of the cost of physical resources. Eventually Froebel 'lost' Music to Southlands, but 'gained' Art from the other colleges. The big prize was Education, which was the last to be rationalised some years later, as it was the largest department, but also the one that represented the ultimate *raison d'être* of all the providing bodies and colleges. It finally became located at Froebel College.

'Rationalisation' (considered at the time as a code for 'centralisation') was an issue that would not go away. Gerald East wrote in November 1983 that 'economic recession and the intransigence of the DES are nagging the Senate and Directorate of Roehampton Institute, along paths which must, it seems, lead eventually to an amalgamation intended to balance the books by rationalising administration'. Even a year later he wrote that 'although we may now hope that we are no longer liable to wake up one morning and find that all our pianos have been requisitioned for transfer to another 'college site' on the say-so of the Senate, the price of federation is nevertheless eternal vigilance'.

Kevin Keohane believed that academic staff were by far the most important resource of an academic institution, and would himself chair all appointment panels for staff wherever possible. To assume, during an interview, that to see him with his eyes shut meant that he was asleep was a big mistake, though he did have a low tolerance for the commonplace and unimaginative. He often said that one rule-of-thumb test of a potential appointee is how would you like to be locked in a carriage with them on the Trans-Siberian Railway? He really did believe that 'a good vacancy is better than a bad appointment'.

In December 1985, Michael Morgan took early retirement, and Jill Redford was appointed in January 1986. She had been Vice-Principal of the West Midlands College of Higher Education and came with a Froebelian heart and CNAA experience. She was a colourful and well-loved person, who could not walk past any person in the college without offering a cheery word. In 1988 the Redford House Nursery was opened on campus, in

The visit of Princess Anne to Froebel College for the Save the Children Fund Fun Day, June 1990

Terry Hewitt, long-serving Deputy Principal

Philip Robinson, eighth Principal of Froebel College

collaboration with Queen Mary's Hospital, helping the College to keep in touch with its Froebelian roots by providing Froebelian day-care for the young children of staff and students at RIHE and the hospital.

In 1986 the Institute had been reorganised into four Faculties, and Jill Redford, as Chair of the Budget Management Group began the process of devolution of financial responsibility to the Faculties. Jill Redford also set up and chaired the Institute's Academic Standards Committee in 1990.

When Kevin Keohane retired in 1988, Professor Stephen Holt was appointed as his successor. He had been Pro-Vice-Chancellor at the University of Kent at Canterbury, and was a political scientist. If Kevin Keohane's task, ably fulfilled, had been to hold the Institute together by keeping the centrifugal forces in check, Stephen Holt's task, again ably fulfilled, was to supervise and co-ordinate the expansion of RIHE and develop its

academic profile and reputation. He persuaded a reluctant Senate in March 1990 that the Institute should 'go modular', and supported Jill Redford's moves to gain 'accreditation' from the University of Surrey in 1992. In 1993 the Institute gained Taught Degree Awarding Powers from the Privy Council, and in 1998 it gained Research Degree Awarding Powers. More than a dozen professors had been appointed, judged against rigorous criteria, and RIHE was now a university in all but name.

Jill Redford took early retirement in 1992, and was succeeded for one year by Terry Hewitt as Acting Principal. A genial and unflappable former FEI Geography lecturer, he had been Deputy Principal since the retirement of Sheila Roberts in 1982. In 1993 the energetic and ambitious Dean of Education, Philip Robinson, was appointed, and held the post for three years before becoming Director of University College Chichester. These years, sadly, saw the deaths of Molly Brearley, in April 1994 at the age of 88, and also of Kevin Keohane in

Dr Kevin Keohane, first Rector of
Roehampton Institute

November 1996, who was only in his mid-seventies. He had died suddenly of a heart attack, and it came as a great shock to his family and all who knew him. St George's Roman Catholic Cathedral, Southwark, was packed to capacity on Friday 8 November, at his memorial service.

Judging that independent university status would make Roehampton too vulnerable to competition from larger London neighbours, and that, as a new university, Roehampton would be in the 'fourth division' according to crude media judgement, Stephen Holt worked towards a federal partnership with an established university. The University of Surrey was the obvious partner. Stephen Holt had already talked informally about a federation with Vice-Chancellor Anthony Kelly in 1988. The catalyst, however, proved to be the enthusiasm and commitment of its next Vice-Chancellor, Professor Patrick Dowling. With the support of the four Providing Bodies of the Roehampton Colleges, of HEFCE and of the DfEE, talks proceeded in earnest through 1998 and 1999. It was to be an *academic* federation, with each of the two constituent partners retaining control of their funding, property, staff appointments and student recruitment.

Professor Stephen Holt, second Rector of
Roehampton Institute

Stephen Holt retired in August 1999, but his successor as Rector, Dr Bernadette Porter, formerly Senior Pro-Rector and Principal of Digby Stuart College, shared the same appreciation of the strategic importance of the Surrey federation to the future of Roehampton and therefore of its constituent colleges. It was to be on Thursday 9th December 1999, as the old century drew to a close that, at a small ceremony in the Senate House of the University of Surrey at Guildford, the Deed of Federation was signed. On 1st January 2000 the new federal institution, **University of Surrey Roehampton**, came into legal existence. On Friday 17th March, 2000, Westminster Abbey was packed with 2000 invited guests to witness the inauguration of this unique federation. One of the readings was from Froebel's book *The Education of Man,* and many former Froebel staff and students were present.

The College had thus survived a turbulent 100 years through being willing to adapt and change. It was now part of the university sector, though at the cost of its independence. The extent to which it remains 'Froebelian' is an issue which the College addresses regularly. The writings of Froebel were steeped in a

Signing of the Deed of Federation, December 1999: (from the left) Dr Elizabeth Nelson (Chair of Roehampton Council), Sir Idris Pearce (Chair of University of Surrey Council), Professor Stephen Holt, Professor Patrick Dowling (Vice-Chancellor of the University of Surrey), and Dr Bernadette Porter (Rector of University of Surrey Roehampton).

WESTMINSTER ABBEY

Service of Thanksgiving and Dedication

to mark the Inauguration of

The University of Surrey Roehampton

as part of

The federal University of Surrey

Friday 17 March 2000

Noon

The Order of Service

In the Jerusalem Chamber, Westminster Abbey, after the Inaugural Service, with the Rev Dr Wesley Carr (Dean of Westminster) and the Duke of Kent (Chancellor of the University of Surrey since 1976)

pattern of thought and articulated in a linguistic idiom and through concepts (such as 'unity') and in contexts (such as 19th-century German nationalism) that were very much of their time and place. But within his writings and practice was a set of values which, when converted into an educational practice appropriate to new times and places, is of enduring importance. These values recognise the individuality of each learner, and oppose the view of the child as an economic 'unit' on whom a rigid curriculum must be imposed, to the detriment of creative expression and joy in learning. If this is utopian, we have to ask why it is. Froebel himself was concerned to protect childhood 'from garments of custom and ancient prescription', and the specific principles and practices deriving from Froebelian values are dynamic and developmental.

The original Froebelian 'missionary' spirit has, necessarily, long since dissipated, and the story of FEI is in part the story of how Froebelian practices and syllabuses have changed and how Froebelian principles have influenced and been assimilated into mainstream educational policy. In some periods, through the 1920s to the 1960s, they were in the ascendant, as witnessed by the Hadow and Plowden Reports, and also by the reminiscences of former students of FEI. In the present, by contrast, they are more 'against the times', and need a stout defence, which is necessary at all stages of the educational process. We believe that the essential Froebelian principles are still present in the Roehampton Early Childhood Studies programmes, in the generic principles of the University's teacher education programmes, and, indeed, it is hoped, in the fabric of College life. A revival of academic interest in Froebel and the kindergarten seems at present to be underway, assisted by easily accessible Internet sources.

The College may now seem to have a relatively secure future as part of a major British university, and, with its partner colleges, be able to influence significant numbers of trainee teachers. If so, it may be said that the next 100 years are a time for reminding the world of the importance of the humane values that Friedrich Froebel devoted his life to promoting. These are based on respect for the uniqueness and wholeness of each individual as a citizen, not merely as a potential employee or consumer, and refusal of the mechanistic, input-output model of education which bureaucrats world-wide usually prefer.

Elements of a Froebelian Education

1. **The Principles include:**
- recognition of the uniqueness of each child's capacity and potential
- a holistic view of each child's development
- an ecological view of mankind in the natural world
- a recognition of the integrity of childhood in its own right
- a recognition of the child as part of the community
- development of all faculties and abilities of each child: imaginative, creative, linguistic, mathematical, musical, aesthetic, scientific, physical, social, moral, cultural and spiritual
- a recognition that parents and educators work in harmony and partnership

2. **The Pedagogy involves:**
- knowledgeable and appropriately qualified teachers and nursery nurses
- awareness that skilled and informed observation of children underpins effective teaching and learning
- use of first hand experience, play, talk and reflection as media for learning
- activities which have sense, purpose and meaning for the child, and involve joy, wonder, concentration, and satisfaction
- a holistic approach to learning which recognises children as active, feeling and thinking human beings, seeing patterns and making connections with their own lives
- encouragement rather than punishment
- individual and collaborative activity and play
- development of children's independence and sense of mastery, building on what children are good at

3. **The Environment should:**
- be physically safe but intellectually challenging, promoting curiosity, enquiry, sensory stimulation and aesthetic awareness
- combine indoors and outdoors, the cultural and the natural
- provide free access to a rich range of materials that promote open-ended opportunities for play, representation and creativity
- demonstrate the nursery to be an integral part of the community it serves, working in close partnership with parents and other skilled adults
- be educative rather than merely amusing or occupying
- promote interdependence as well as independence, community as well as individuality and responsibility as well as freedom.

OUTLINE CHRONOLOGY

1837	'Play and Activity Institute' established by Friedrich Froebel in Bad Blankenburg
1840	Renamed 'Kindergarten'
1851	*August: The Kindergartenverbot* closes all kindergartens in Prussia, followed by Bavaria and other German states and Swiss Cantons
	September: The first kindergarten in England established in Hampstead
1852	*June:* death of Friedrich Froebel
1870	Elementary Education Act ('Forster' Act) establishes first national system of education in England and Wales, managed by School Boards
1872	Girls' Public Day School Company established
1873	Mrs Salis-Schwabe establishes kindergarten & school in Naples
1874	*November:* Froebel Society established
1879	*Easter:* Kindergarten Training College established in Tavistock Place
1883	*July:* Kindergarten Training College closes through lack of funds
1884	Froebel Society Council established (secretary Claude Montefiore)
1887	June: National Froebel Union established
1892	*October:* Froebel Educational Institute constituted (chairman William Mather, treasurer Claude Montefiore)
1893	Colet Gardens site acquired and building commences
	January: death of Baroness von Marenholtz-Bülow
1894	*January:* FEI College building (Colet Gardens) occupied
	March: formal opening of Colet Gardens by HIM the Empress Frederick
1896	*May:* death of Mrs Salis-Schwabe
	July: Demonstration School wing opened, headmistress Esther Lawrence
	September: Michaelis Guild established
1899	*November:* Practising School opened in Challoner Street
1900	*January:* death of Froebel's second wife, Luise Levin
	FEI incorporated as IFEI, a 'company not for gain'
1901	*March:* Mme Michaelis resigns
	September: Esther Lawrence becomes Principal, Miss Yelland Headmistress
1902	The 'Balfour' Act replaces School Boards with LEAs
1904	*December:* death of Mme Michaelis
1916	*April:* death of Miss Yelland
1917	Sir William Mather retires as Chairman of FEI; succeeded by Claude Montefiore
1918	The 'Fisher' Act introduces free and compulsory education to age 14
1920	*September:* death of Sir William Mather
	FEI formally recognised by Board of Education, making students eligible for grants

1921	First FEI hostel opened in Gliddon Road
	August: Grove House, with 33 acres, purchased
	'Temporary' bungalows built on Grove House lawn, including three lecture rooms, to house 80 students
1922	*January:* Grove House occupied
	February: Queen Mary visits Grove House
1923	Lulham building opened
1926	New Court residences opened
1927	Grove House dining room (now Portrait Room) extended, with rooms above
1928	Row (now Redford House Nursery) opened
	September: Grove House School opened
1929	NFU recognised by Board of Education as eligible to confer qualified teacher status; Art Room opened
	November: Templeton occupied
1931	*December:* Miss Lawrence retires
1932	Miss Jebb appointed as Principal
1933	The Hadow Report on Infant and Nursery Schools endorses Froebelian principles
1933-1934	Dry rot in Grove House repaired
1934	Death of Miss Lulham
1938	Claude Montefiore resigns as Chairman of FEI; succeeded in 1939 by Leonard, his son
	June: Lawrence Building and Montefiore Wing opened, replacing 'bungalows'
	July: death of Claude Montefiore
	The Froebel Society and the National Froebel Union merge to form the National Froebel Foundation
1939	Evacuation of Grove House to Knebworth and Offley Place, Hertfordshire
	Evacuation of Colet Gardens School to Little Gaddesden, Hertfordshire
	Grove House School closes
1943	FEI purchases Offley Place
1944	The 'Butler' Act provides for secondary education for all, the eleven plus, and a Ministry of Education to control LEAs
	The McNair Report recommends Area Training Organisations based on University Schools of Education, and a three-year training course
	July: death of Miss Lawrence
1945	Return to Grove House, but Offley Place retained
1946	Ibstock Place School opens, and Colet Gardens sold to Sadlers Wells Ballet
1950	*September:* First cohort of FEI students registers for *both* the NFF Teacher's Certificate *and* the University of London Institute of Education Teacher's Certificate
1953	Offley Place sold to Hertfordshire LEA

1954	*June:* death of Miss Venour, former Warden of Offley Place Training College
1955	Miss Jebb retires; succeeded by Molly Brearley as Principal; Grove House listed Grade II*
1957	Death of Mr Longhurst, Grove House gardener
1958	*February:* Opening of Michaelis building
1960	*September:* Three-year teacher training courses introduced nationally
1961	Death of Leonard Montefiore, Chairman of FEI; succeeded by Joyce Bishop
1962	*May:* Opening of Leonard Montefiore Hall & Dining Room, Education Block, and Jebb House residences
1963	The Newsom Report recommends training for all graduate entrants to teaching
	The Robbins Report renames training colleges 'Colleges of Education' and recommends that they offer a four-year BEd degree
1965	*September:* first male students enter FEI
1966	The Weaver Report recommends composition of college governing bodies
	Anthony Crosland invents the term 'the public sector' for polytechnics and colleges
1967	The Plowden Report affirms the principles of child-centred education; opening of Olive Garnett building, Music rooms, and Garden Court (residences)
	September: first entrants to BEd degree at FEI
1969	FEI adopts a new constitution comprising a Council of Management with a separate Governing Body for the College, both chaired by Dame Joyce Bishop
1970	Molly Brearley retires; succeeded by Priscilla Steele as Principal
1971-1973	Informal discussions with neighbouring colleges about federation, in anticipation of the James Report and drastic reductions in teacher training numbers
1972-1973	Priscilla Steele on sick leave; the College managed by Deputy Principal, Lewis Howdle, and the 'Junta'
1972	*January:* The James Report proposes sequential cycles of education and training, 2-A-level entry, the DipHE, and 3-year degree courses for colleges of education
	June: The first meeting between Principals of the four Colleges at FEI
	December: the White Paper *Education: a Framework for Expansion* foresees a reduction in teacher training numbers
1973	*August:* Priscilla Steele resigns; Lewis Howdle Acting Principal for one year
	November: A 'Statement of Intent' to form an 'Association' submitted to DES
1974	*January:* The Formation Committee meets for the first time and the Planning Body [JIAPB] set up, both soon to be chaired by Dr James Topping, to agree terms and structures for the establishment of Roehampton Institute of Higher Education
	January: Proposals for diversified courses submitted to London University Institute of Education
	August: Michael Morgan appointed Principal
	Dame Joyce Bishop retires as Chair of FEI Council of Management and of College Governing Body;

	succeeded in 1975 by Alan Montefiore, son of Leonard
1975	*July:* Secretary of State Fred Mulley approves the establishment of RIHE
	September: First students admitted on non-teacher training degree courses
1976	First Rector of RIHE, Dr Kevin Keohane, appointed
1977	Early Childhood Archive [now 'Froebel Archive for Childhood Studies'] established
1978	*May:* death of Miss Jebb
1979	All College staff transferred to payroll of RIHE
	Alan Montefiore resigns as Chair of FEI Council of Management and of College Governing Body; succeeded by Gerald East
1981	FEI adopts new Constitution, with a Council, College Governing Body, School Governing Body and Research Committee
	Rory Hands becomes Chair of College Governing Body
	Last students admitted to courses validated by the University of London
1982	First entrants to University of Surrey degree courses at RIHE
1985	*December:* Michael Morgan retires early
1986	*January:* Jill Redford appointed as Principal
1988	Kevin Keohane retires; succeeded by Professor Stephen Holt as Rector
1989	Gerald East resigns as Chair of FEI Council; succeeded by Rory Hands
	Rory Hands resigns as Chair of College Governors; succeeded by Mary Henderson
1991	*September:* First entry to modular degree programmes
1992	*August:* Jill Redford retires early; Terry Hewitt Acting Principal for one year
1993	Philip Robinson appointed Principal
	Mary Henderson resigns as Chair of College Governors; succeeded by Kenneth Philpot
	June: death of Dame Joyce Bishop, age 96
	RIHE gains Taught Degree Awarding Powers from the Privy Council
1994	*March:* death of Molly Brearley
	Rory Hands resigns as Chair of FEI Council; succeeded by Richard Hastie Smith
1996	*April:* Philip Robinson resigns; succeeded by Dr Peter Weston as Principal
	November: death of Kevin Keohane
1998	RIHE [now RIL – Roehampton Institute London] gains Research Degree Awarding Powers from the Privy Council
1999	Stephen Holt retires; succeeded by Dr Bernadette Porter as Rector
2000	*January:* The University of Surrey Roehampton established
	March: The University of Surrey Roehampton inaugurated in Westminster Abbey
2001	*December:* death of Stephen Holt

ACKNOWLEDGEMENTS

The author thanks in particular Dr John Seed, for his helpful and encouraging comments on an early draft of this text; Sheila Campbell, who has served four Principals (and one Acting Principal) as PA, for her reliable and professional work; and also Sheila Roberts and Jane Read for their support in different ways. I am grateful also to Mrs Howdle and Alan Montefiore for the loan of certain photographs.

I have found four other college histories of particular interest, two of which were Froebel colleges: Irene Lilley's *Maria Grey College 1878-1976* (Twickenham, 1981), Richard Smart's *Bedford Training College 1882-1982* (Bedford, 1982), G.P. McGregor's *A Church College for the 21st Century? 150 years of Ripon & York St John* (York, 1991), and Douglas Milbank's *Years of Change: a History of Southlands College, 1970-1985* (Roehampton Institute, undated). In addition, Roy Douglas's *Surrey the Rise of a Modern University* (Guildford, 1991), and Negley Harte's *The University of London 1836-1986* (London, 1986) were useful sources of information. The standard contemporary polemic on the dissolution of the Colleges of Education is David Hencke's *Colleges in Crisis* (Harmondsworth, 1978). Otherwise most of the raw data on which the research is based are to be found in the Froebel Archive for Childhood Studies at Froebel College, SW15, or in the National Froebel Foundation Archive at Templeton, SW15, headquarters of FEI.

A very significant debt is owed to the many former students, all members of the Froebel Guild, who in 2000 submitted their reminiscences of the College for the Froebel Archive at the author's request, and who are listed below. Their memories have added a personal flavour to the research, and I am only sorry that their contributions to this book have been limited by inevitable pressures of space and cost.

Jo Parker (1923-26), Christine Carpenter (1924-27), Kathleen Lulman (1925-28), Janet Park (1928-30), Mary Stone (1928-31), Marjorie Fletcher (1930-33), Frances Ginger (1930-33), Rosemary Hewett (1930-33), Marion Honey (1930-33), Helen Tyack (1930-33), Barbara West (1930-33), Sylvia Bandy (1931-34), Patricia Berryman (1931-34), Joyce Cooper (1931-35), Joyce Hoyle (1932-35), Eileen Morris (1932-35), Eileen Humphrey (1933-36), Elizabeth Lawrence (1933-36), Elizabeth Woolnough (1933-36), L.E. Facey (1934-37), Katie Heywood (1934-37), Joan Forsyth (1935-38), Sister Barbara Griffiths & Catharine Crawford (1935-38), Margaret Pope (1935-38), Catherine Roulet (1935-38), Elizabeth Fraser (1936-39), Jean Gill (1936-39), Gabrielle Merritt (1936-39), Val Wight-Boycott (1936-39), Diana Loy (1937-40), Patricia Bigg (1937-40), Olive Pain (1937-40), Christine Trodd (1937-40), Peggy Cocks (1938-41), Diana Goodhart (1938-41), Mary Humfrey (1938-41), Margaret Kerr (1938-41), Sylvia Montgomery (1938-41), J.C.O. Ray (1938-41), Margaret Rushby (1938-41), Iris Appleton (1939-42), Helen Cook (1939-42), Margaret Hillidie Smith (1939-42), Elizabeth Millman (1939-42), M.J. Smith (1939-42), Marion Hemidge (1940s), Ann Cubitt (1940-43), Patience Beale (1941-43), Trudie Morrish (1941-43), Eleanor Bennett (1941-44), Deirdre Clarke (1941-44), Myrtle Ellenbogen (1941-44), Brenda Blake (1942-44), Jill Craig (1942-44), Stella Bryant (1942-45), Sheila Mortimer (1942-45), Ruth Barnish (1943-46), Catherine Giles (1943-46), Velma Krever (1943-46), Ilse Perlmutter (1943-46), Patience Bagerel (1944-47), Anne Furber (1944-47), Mary Miles (1944-47), Katherine Robertson (1944-47), Wendy Vachell (1945-47), Anne Stammers (1945-48), Barbara Bunton (1945-48), Joan Dickins (1945-48), Mavis Ingham (1945-48), Elizabeth Traill (1945-63), Naomi Ashton (1946-49), Mary Dixey (1946-49), Diana Gibson (1946-49), Kay Hassell (1946-49), E.J. Lines (1946-49), Mary Bedford (1948-51), R. Chevallier (1948-51), Mary Hickmott (1948-51), Betty Palmer (1948-51), Ruth Westover (1948-51), Janet Wilmshurst (1948-51), Valerie Dewhurst (1949-51), B. Butterworth (1949-52), Gillian Hall (1949-52), Betty Staff (1949-52), Carolyn Hambidge (1950s), J.M. Goswell (1952-55), Beryl Hussey (1952-55), Rhiannon Reddin (1952-55), Delyn Williams (1952-55), Shirley Boyce (1953-56), Tessa Morgan (1953-56), F.S. Milner (1954-56), Sylvia Clements (1954-57), Anne Coombe (1954-57), Pamela Dixon (1954-57), Shelagh Jenkyns (1954-57), Mary Perrins (1954-57), Kate Pontifex (1954-57), G.B. Oshinowo (1955-58), Mary Vallance (1955-58), Leslie Forward (1956-78), Mary Roosevelt (1957-60), E.M. Stokes (1957-60), Lynne Bartholomew (1958-61), J.M. Davies (1958-61), Wendy Scott (1958-61), Annabelle Dixon (1959-62), Sarah Coe (1960s), Lynette Gribble (1960-63), Rosemary Morgan (1960-63), Megan Warner (1961-64), Ann Edmonds (1962-65), Sue Pierson (1962-65), Jean Reed (1962-65), Elizabeth Vaughan (1962-65), Judy Hargreaves (1964-67), Kathleen Sanderson (1965-68), Rose Williams (1966-69), Nancy Vlasto (1969-72), Jenny Casboult (1969-73)

INDEX

References in **_bold italics_** indicate illustrations